MW00399458

DAWNING *of a* NEW DAY

A JOURNEY OUT OF DARKNESS

by

Carolyn M. DeLeon

INKWATER PRESS

Copyright © 2004 by Carolyn M. DeLeon

All rights reserved. No part of this book may be reproduced or transmitted in any form or by any means whatsoever, including photocopying, recording or by any information storage and retrieval system, without written permission from the publisher. Contact Inkwater Press at 6750 SW Franklin Street, Suite A, Portland, OR 97223.

www.inkwaterpress.com

ISBN 1-59299-054-1

Publisher: Inkwater Press

Printed in the U.S.A.

All scripture text for Dawning of a New Day is taken from *The Life Application Bible: New International Version Bible* (NIV). Copyright 1988, 1989, 1990, 1991, published jointly by Tyndale House Publishers and Zondervan Publishing House.

Dedication

In memory of David... your life truly counted and touched many
In memory of Colleen Marie Kilmer-Stone... the burning flame of
your life was quenched too early
To Corrie who inspired me with the idea to write this book
To my family who loved me unconditionally
To the many suicide survivors... may you find peace

Acknowledgments

I would like to thank the many people who supported and encouraged the writing of this book. Thank you to my parents Ron and Debe, my brothers Ron and Eric, for your love, support and encouragement. Thank you to my pastors Dan and Kathy Greenlee, you are true shepherds in the Kingdom of God. Thank you to Pastors Bob and MaryEllen Shafer, for your unconditional love and the many hours of prayer that were deposited into my life. Thank you to Corrie Marcellino, for the countless hours of wise counseling.

Thank you to Bobby Clinton, for your wisdom and guidance and for not giving up after the first reading of this manuscript. You are all true blessings in my life.

Table of Contents

Foreword

Dawning of a New Day is a book of redemption written out of deep pain and tragedy. It's much more than theory; it's the reality of life.

Life throws us challenges and tragedies that are so unfair, yet God's redeeming grace can penetrate the darkest hour and bring new tomorrows, new dreams, and new hopes. As Carolyn's pastor I had the opportunity of watching her walk through the most difficult pain of her life into a new day. I knew that my words were so limited and that eventually only God could do the impossible: heal a broken heart and restore shattered dreams. Yet, wonderfully it happened. Not over night, not without pain and anguish, not without struggle, yet is happening.

Some may find Carolyn's insights painfully honest, because she didn't retreat into patterns of denial. She faced her pain, her fears and anguish. Although God seemed so distant, she hung on to her faith and ultimate confidence in the Father's character.

Weeping does endure for a night, but joy will come in the morning. There are times of weeping and pain, but they won't last forever. This book looks beyond the season of pain and embraces the hope of the "morning." I believe this book will be a tool of healing and hope for those who must face similar tragedies and pain. God really can redeem the pain of our lives (2 Cor. 1:3-4).

What a wonderful God we have. He is the Father of our Lord Jesus Christ, the Source of every mercy, and the One Who so wonderfully comforts and strengthens us in our hardships and trials. And why does He do this? So that when others are troubled, needing our sympathy and encouragement, we can pass on to them this same help and comfort God has given us (TLB).

— Dr. Daniel Greenlee, Pastor
The Father's House International

Preface

I have been a grief counselor for over twenty-five years. People continually ask me, "How do you do this work? Isn't it depressing? All you see is grieving people."

Sometimes, I must admit, that I ask myself the same questions. But always, an answer quickly comes. I am blessed to do this work. I am blessed to be able to accompany a person through an often dark night of the soul on their path of grief. I do see a lot of sadness, but I also see an equal amount of courage, hope, and healing. And it is most definitely the gifts of people like Carolyn DeLeon that allows me to carry the faith and hope for others when theirs is lacking; and the belief that they too will heal if they allow grief to move in its own unique way.

Being a witness to Carolyn's journey of grief was, and continues to be a powerful and inspiring experience for me, both professionally and personally. I am most pleased that she has chosen to share some of her most intimate details of her journey along grief's often rocky road. I trust that her words will touch countless others who are experiencing many of the same feelings, and be a lamp of hope on a dark and frightening journey that those who have lost a loved one to suicide know all too well.

I have witnessed Carolyn move through her grief with sadness, despair, questions, faith, honesty, and courage. I have been given the opportunity to watch as she has stepped back into life again with a new clarity and strength of faith and most certainly a powerful and important story to tell.

— Corrie Marcellino, LCSW
Former Director of Social Services and Bereavement, Hospice of the Valley, San Jose, CA

Introduction

In writing Dawning of a New Day: A Journey Out of Darkness, Carolyn DeLeon has followed 2 Corinthians 1:3,4.

> God should be honored as the Father of our
> Lord Jesus Christ, a merciful Father and the
> God who comforts. He comforts us in all
> our trying experiences. Then we in turn can
> comfort those facing like trying experiences
> with the help we have received from God.

Carolyn has faced a very trying experience and known the comfort of God. Now she is helping others to learn about the comfort of the Father. She has written her own personal book of 2 Corinthians. When the trying experiences of life come, and they come to all, they are God's way of calling us into a deeper relationship with Himself. I have observed that two things can happen to people at these times. Some go deep with God. Others turn away from God. Carolyn has gone deep with God.

The grieving process has been long and deep.

Carolyn discovered her own approach to grieving, and she tells us about it by using clear and forceful language. She sometimes quotes tidbits from others that have helped her to grasp meaning during this time: poems, mini-illustrations, conversations, and her own personal journal entries. These journal entries are a particular strength of her work. We learn not only the what of her experience, but a way of dealing with deep processing. Her images and metaphors also capture the intensity of her grieving and of her release from grieving.

This is one of the most powerful images, the 'Good-bye image,' of Chapter 8. I include it here because these words beautifully describe what Carolyn does for us in this book. We see both the pain involved in grief, and the choices that one must make in order to turn and walk on in life.

> When I think about 'the act' of saying good-bye to someone, we both stand facing each other waving and saying good-bye. It is not until one actually turns and begins walking away that one gets anywhere. Similarly, I have stood stationary with tears streaming down my face, waving and saying good-bye, long enough. I have turned. God has wiped the tears from my eyes, my vision is clearing, and I am beginning to walk down my own path in life. Turning brought pain; taking the first step brought agony. Now with every little step I take, it becomes less painful and more hopeful for the future.

Carolyn's intimate reflections in her journal and her personal experiences help us all to understand that this journey is difficult, can be long, and is always full of questions. We see too, that the asking of questions, and the expression of emotion is an important part of the grieving process. She exposes her feelings of guilt. She is angry with God. She talks about blame, which can be devastating for a suicide survivor because the questions are different when someone chooses their own death. Her honesty is helpful as she shares her struggles with faith issues and talks about extreme isolation-her feelings of abandonment by God. She questions God with the honesty of Job.

In the last part of her book she talks about the importance of ritual. She has begun her own traditions to capture and express her emotion and choices. She tells you of the importance of memories and a final goodbye. Once again, her personal sharing helps each of us ask the questions that we need in order to find our own unique ways of turning and walking on, no matter what the loss is that we each face. And then finally, she faces the future, as a single, resolutely and yet with careful reflective thought. It is a new day for her.

This book is important because she is dealing with an untouchable grief. That of a suicide survivor. In the church for too long now, we have insulated ourselves from the pain of suicide survivors by isolating them at the very times when they need us the most. In the church we can do this because of our own unanswered questions, thoughts, and feelings, which make us feel inadequate to help.

Sometimes we isolate suicide survivors because of our pat solutions and ready answers which don't make sense when one has gone through such deep sorrow. Carolyn's book can help those who are working with suicide survivors, and the survivors themselves.

Like Paul, Carolyn is open, transparent and vulnerable. She holds nothing back. This book is the story of her grief and comfort. May her new day give hope for others who face deep processing. May they too learn the shaping activity of God. Don't ignore the Appendix. Those suggestions are valuable.

Bobby Clinton
Professor of Leadership
Fuller Theological Seminary

Chapter One

The First Day

I am in pain and distress.
May your salvation, O God, protect me.
— Psalm 69:29

On Monday, August 12, 1996, my husband David committed suicide. I came home and found him dead in his wheelchair.

I have never experienced such horror and trauma. Looking back now, I can see that he had thoughts of suicide long before he ever completed the act, but still it shattered me. His death left me disillusioned, angry, disoriented with life and especially with God. As we were committed Christians, I did not understand why he took his life. My perception of a strong marriage and a good life no longer existed. My world lay in pieces.

Before David's suicide I developed a daily spiritual devotion of writing during my prayer time; and since the day of his suicide I have kept a personal journal of my thoughts and struggles as I traveled from complete devastation, brokenness, shattered emotions, and what I considered lost faith. I have come to a new place of restoration, emotional healing, and newfound faith. This is my testimony of a journey complete yet one just beginning.

The weekend before David's suicide felt crazy and difficult. We argued about everything. We could not have a calm conversation. We could not pray, laugh, or anything else we usually did. I knew something bothered him, but he would not tell me what. I finally gave up trying to talk to him. Instead, I asked God to show me the cause and what I should do. Our relationship had never come to such a difficult place before. I basically left him alone in bed, or we sat in opposite ends of the house.

On that Monday morning, the day he killed himself, I got up earlier than usual and went to work earlier than normal just to get out of the house.

Waking up that morning, I thought, *God, what can we do to make things different? How can I approach David, and how can we begin to talk and pray again?*

I showered and sipped my morning cup of coffee. I stood in front of the kitchen sink and stared out the window. Looking across the street at the neighbors' houses and gazing into the blue sky, I wondered how God would help us through this difficult time.

I went into our bedroom. It was dark from the curtains still being drawn. I had turned David on his side when I first got up to relieve the pressure from lying flat on his back all night. The extent of David's disability was quadriplegia which did not allow him to move.

I went in to turn him back at 7:30 in the morning. Our attendant had not arrived yet. When I turned him,

I felt tense and nervous because I did not want to start an argument.

David looked at me and said in a rather monotone voice, "Don't worry about coming home early or hurrying to finish your work at the end of the day. Just take your time today. Don't look at the clock, and don't feel like you have to rush home."

I said, "Okay, I'll see you when I get home," thinking in my mind, *Thank God, things are changing and we'll be able to talk and pray when I get home today.*

I felt relieved at the sense of the tension breaking — finally. I didn't kiss him good-bye or tell him that I loved him.

I simply said, "I'll see you when I get home."

I left for work and had a busy day. I ate lunch with a colleague, and we talked about the difficulty David and I were having. Usually when my day at work is busy, I become stressed out and anxious, but on that day I had peace. It was unusual.

I left work about 5:45 p.m., and traffic was heavy that evening.

Sitting there in the middle of it, my thoughts drifted, and I prayed silently, *God, what is it that has been causing us so much stress and strain? What can I do to help make things different, to bring about change for the better? Should we go away for a while, just the two of us? Should I take a week off work and just spend it with David?*

While praying, I felt God's presence surrounding me. The strength of His presence made me not want to move. It felt as if I was wrapped tightly in a blanket. It

3

seemed a little odd, because I had never felt God's Spirit surround me like that before.

"Thank you, Lord," I whispered. "You're telling me that You know what is happening and You're going to do something to help us."

I felt even more peace.

I finally got onto the freeway and continued my drive home. Arriving about 6:30, I opened the automatic garage door, drove in, and parked my car. I got out, closed the garage door, then went into the house through the laundry room and into the family room.

Turning to the right and looking into the kitchen, I saw the house was dark. The blinds were shut in the kitchen and the drapes closed in the family room. It seemed strange to me, because I had opened them before leaving. Walking through the kitchen, I glanced at the telephone on the kitchen counter. The red light on the phone was shining, which meant someone was on the phone in our bedroom.

At that moment I thought I heard David talking to someone. I did not hear anything specific, but because I heard his voice, I did not go into our room right away. I thought he was talking on the phone and did not want to interrupt his conversation.

I walked to the bathroom and washed my hands, then went to the front door to get the mail. I noticed that the front door was locked, and a strange feeling came over me. I never locked it during the day when David was home, in case of an emergency if other people had to get in. Though it was strange, I dismissed it, thinking maybe our attendant accidentally locked it when he left that morning.

I came back in and went into the kitchen, sifting through the mail. Glancing over the counter, I noticed David's afternoon medication had not been taken yet, but the glass of water I left for him was gone. Looking in the refrigerator, I noticed his dinner still there.

I walked back through the kitchen and turned left down the hallway toward our bedroom, where the door hung open a crack. It had a string attached to the doorknob and a nail on the wall, so David could open and close the door easily. Slowly I pushed open the door and looked down the narrow hallway with two large closets on the right and a sliding glass door on the left. The end of the hallway opened up to a large master bedroom with a walk in vanity area and bathroom.

Standing at the end of the hallway, I saw David sitting at his desk — a large drafting table set up for his wheelchair to fit underneath. His Bible was open on his bookstand as normal, but I noticed his head tilted down and to the left. I thought he had fallen asleep.

I saw our dog Jacob lying behind the wheelchair. Jacob did not move when I came into the room, which was unusual for him. Instead, he stayed lying down and looked up at me with his big brown eyes.

"David," I called out.

He did not move.

Walking down the hallway toward him I called his name again.

"David."

He still did not move. I felt bad, because I thought he became tired and had to wait for me to get home to put him in bed.

Coming to the back of his wheelchair, I stretched out my hand, called his name a little more loudly, and touched the back of his neck. It was cold and stiff....

"*No!*" I screamed. "David!"

I knew instantly he had committed suicide.

As soon as he heard my outcry, Jacob slowly got up and walked down the hallway.

"Oh, my God!" I screamed out loud. "What did I do to you?"

My whole body trembled from confusion and fear. A million thoughts raced through my head.

What do I do? My husband is dead. Who do I call?

Going to the left side of his wheelchair, I put my right hand on the back of his head and my left hand on the front of his forehead. As I lifted his head, his whole body moved back, because he had been dead for several hours.

Looking at his face, I burst into tears. His color was ashen gray, his face drawn, and his eyes wide open — bulging from the sockets. Saliva mixed with foam and blood dripped from his mouth. His facial expression was that of nausea, vomiting. The one arm of which he had movement, his right, appeared frozen on the right wheelchair arm with his wrist flexed in an upward position.

I could not believe what I saw.

I said aloud, "I need to call someone. Yeah, I need to call someone. Nine-one-one."

Looking over at the phone on the desk, I noticed the receiver was off the hook. The cord with the receiver was wrapped around David's right arm and the right wheelchair arm, running across his lap, around his left arm, and hanging down the left side of his wheelchair.

Shaking badly, I unwrapped the telephone cord from his body. Things moved in slow motion. When I finally got the cord free, I called 911.

"I need help. My husband is dead. He killed himself."

The male operator responded, "You need to check and see if he is breathing, and we need to do CPR on him."

"Trust me!" I yelled. "We don't need to do CPR on him. He is very cold, very stiff, and very dead!"

"Hold on, ma'am. The fire department, police, and paramedics are on the way."

Listening to the operator, although oblivious to his words, I stared at my husband.

Gazing around on his desk, I noticed the missing glass of water from the kitchen sitting there with powder residue inside the empty cup. Behind his Bible stand I saw the five bottles of prescription drugs I had just refilled for him, with the caps bitten off the tops of the bottles. Scanning the room, I noticed the stereo was on. He must have been playing the praise and worship music I put in the CD player the night before. I saw the Bible opened to the book of Proverbs.

After looking around, I sank down against the wall just looking at David — his open eyes staring right through me. Shock and guilt resounded through my body.

Still holding the receiver, listening to the rambling words of the operator, I did not really process what he said. It seemed as if hours had passed, though in reality it was only a few minutes until the firefighters, paramedics, and police arrived.

They came in and down the hallway to our bedroom. The lead man was wearing plastic gloves. Moving close to David, he took one look at him, looked at me, looked down, and took off his gloves. Turning around, he said something to the others on their way down the hall. The rush and urgency abruptly changed to slow, somber movement.

A female paramedic took me out of the bedroom and back into the kitchen.

People fired question after question.

"Do you have anyone you can call?"

"Do you know the telephone numbers?"

"What time did you get home?"

"Did you touch anything in the bedroom?"

"Who was the last person with your husband?"

"Where is your phone book?"

"I'll call the people for you. Who do you want me call?"

A firefighter dialed my mom for me.

"Mom?" I said.

"What's wrong?" she asked.

"Mom, David killed himself."

"I'll be right there."

She lived over forty minutes away but arrived in fifteen.

The firefighter also called my father-in-law. I did not tell him anything on the phone. He had a bad heart, and I did not want anything to happen to him on the way over.

"Something has happened to David," I said, "and you need to come over right now."

My mom had her friend call my younger brother, and he called my dad and the rest of my family. I don't know who called my pastor, but he came as well.

I went back into my bedroom — walking in shock, crying, sweating, shaking. I stood in disbelief that my husband had committed suicide.

Standing there staring at him, I thought, *Is my husband in hell because he took his own life?*

I stood there lost in such thoughts until I heard someone walk up behind me. It was my pastor. Looking at me, then over at David, then back at me, he had tears in his eyes.

I said, "He killed himself."

He looked at me. "You have to know that this has no bearing on eternity."

I was relieved to hear him say that. It was the most important thing anyone could have said to me at that moment.

He and I walked out back, away from all the people, and talked for a while. I don't recall what he said, but he was shocked too. We went into the kitchen, and I asked him to pray for me. He prayed a short prayer, then left. I knew there was nothing anyone could do for me at the time except to be with me.

Now I was standing in the living room. Someone took me by the shoulders and turned me around to sit in a chair. Glancing over my shoulder, I saw the coroner taking David's body out on a gurney, zipped in a black bag. My shock went deeper; my numbness increased.

My cousin came over and acted as if she did not know what to do.

Looking at her, I said, "I need a glass of wine, something to relax. Will you go to the cabinet and pour me a glass of wine?"

She did not hesitate, even though she knew I did not drink.

Sitting out front on the lawn, I consumed two glasses of wine. As I finished the second glass, my friend and colleague from work, Anita, arrived. I became anxious, so we took a walk around the block. She stayed for several hours.

My mom was still there resting on the living room couch. After the paramedics, firefighters, and police left, others trickled out as well. Anita left because she had to work the next morning, and it was already the early-morning hours.

My mom took me to her house. She asked if I was going to be all right, I told her yes, and she went to bed.

I went into the guest room, lay down on the bed, and wept. My eyes were swollen and red from crying so much. After glancing at the clock — 3:30 a.m. — I must have fallen asleep briefly, because when I looked at the clock again, it was 4:15. I was wide awake.

Looking around, I realized that I was not at home, and the memories came flooding back.

David is dead.

I began crying again. I got up and made a pot of coffee, thinking if I was up all hours of the morning and night, I might as well enjoy a good cup of coffee. I sat in the family room in a recliner chair with my legs crossed Indian-style and a blanket covering my lap.

The depth of my shock made my thoughts spin around in my head. I could not stop them.

I'm scared. Why did he kill himself? What did I do to make him do that? It's my fault. I didn't tell him I loved him. Maybe he wouldn't have killed himself if I had said I loved him or given him a kiss good-bye. Why didn't I kiss him good-bye? He's gone, and I'm never going to see him again. He was in so much pain, and I wasn't there to help him. I didn't help him. Why didn't I know or sense something was going to happen? Oh, my God, what am I going to do?

Cast into the beginning of a journey through grief and mourning, I thought I would not survive.

> Everything that has happened just seems so impossible, but it's actually true. My husband, the one I loved most in the world, committed suicide, and he's gone now. Forever gone from my life on this Earth. I don't have any peace. I can't think clearly.
> Where is God? I need God.
>
> Journal Entry,
> August 16, 1996

Chapter Two

My Story

As the deer pants for streams
of water, so my soul pants for you,
O' God. My soul thirsts for God, for the Living God.
When can I go and meet with God?

— Psalm 42:1-2

His death certificate reads: *Death by lethal ingestion of prescribed drugs — suicide.*

I constantly ask myself, *Why? What made him commit suicide? What drove him to the edge of despair where he felt no hope? Why did God let it happen without warning me? Did I do something that made him kill himself?*

It has been seven years, and I have asked myself these questions a thousand times. My husband's suicide lingers as a legacy of unanswered questions — and although I haven't found any answers, I have found peace.

I believe God can answer all my questions, but even if He did, it would not remove the pain. My pain, anger, depression, guilt, and shame were unbearable at times.

I said over and over, "I'm not going to make it."

I did make it, although I had a long, slow-healing journey, and my healing continues. I realized that by God's grace, strength, and faithfulness through the grief, healing and the dawning of a new day come after one of life's most tragic events — the suicide of a spouse.

When suicide strikes our lives in a way we never dream about, how do we as suicide survivors, walk through the ensuing intense journey of grief and healing? How do others respond to suicide survivors? What can be done to help survivors walk through the different seasons of grief?

To the many suicide survivors walking through a similar grieving and healing journey, I share my intimate moments. I share my insights and realizations to give a voice to your grief and remove the sense of aloneness. I pray you receive hope, find peace, and gain a sense of perspective as you walk through your journey of grief after suicide.

While reading this book I hope you gain awareness that, "Grief has purpose. It is a passageway, of sorts, from one form of life to another, a journey that must be traveled."[1] By my opening my personal world of tragedy, pain, and healing, may it give you assurance that you can make it through the circumstance life has brought your way.

Here is my story.

In 1980, while out with a friend, a man shot David in the neck, and it paralyzed him instantly. The shooter was caught and sentenced to seven years in prison, then released. David, however, received a life sentence of quadriplegia. His severe spinal-cord injury left him with chronic pain — a constant burning sensation and shoot-ing pain throughout his body. He took medication daily, but the strongest medications gave him little relief.

I met David in 1987. My grandmother introduced us. She visited David every Saturday as part of her min-istry service, and one Saturday afternoon I went with her to meet him.

David came out from his room, and I thought, *This man is handsome. Too bad he's in a wheelchair.*

He was six feet tall and sat in his wheelchair with astuteness. His dark brown hair was always perfectly combed. His dark eyelashes and eyebrows accentuated his hazel eyes and ivory skin. His eyes changed to green or light brown depending on the color of clothing he wore. His was voice deep and pleasant. A peacefulness within his spirit emanated through his eyes.

We spent several hours talking that day and be-came friends quickly. We discovered we had a lot in common, most important our faith in Jesus. We both enjoyed studying the Bible and talking about what God was doing in our lives.

We liked watching Monday night football and ana-lyzing the plays as if we could go out on the field and do better. His favorite team was the Forty-Niners, mine the Chicago Bears. We liked nice cars and enjoyed driving. We liked being outdoors and going to the park or the beach.

Our favorite place was the beach over on the Monterey coast. A certain section of pavement allowed David to get close to the water in his wheelchair, so that we could close our eyes, hold hands, listen to the waves washing on the shore, and imagine ourselves walking along the beach. David told me frequently how much he wanted to walk with me hand in hand along the beach.

He was romantic! He bought me flowers, always a dozen red roses. He loved taking me to different places, and while we were out, he always put his arm around me. He wanted people to know we were together and that I was not otherwise available.

Our friendship and intimacy deepened. Our time together strengthened and solidified our love. We spent hours talking, enjoying one another's company, and valuing each other's opinions and ideas.

Over three years our love and friendship grew. David was a man of faith, courage, and strength. He prayed and believed God to heal other people. When tragedies came to others, he supported them, called them, and gave what he could. He was sensitive, caring, and loving, not only with me but others. His compassion for people transcended his own pain and needs. On days when he experienced excruciating pain, he prayed and spoke encouraging words to others. Any need that David could meet, he did not hesitate in providing. He gave.

I remember thinking one day, *I love this man,* and I knew that he loved me.

In April 1990, while we were sitting and talking, he gazed into my eyes and said, "I love you. Will you marry me?"

He added, "I would get down on one knee, but given the circumstances you have to accept the proposal with me sitting down."

Part of me wanted to say yes, but another part of me thought, *I can't do this. He's in a wheelchair.*

I told him that I loved him but did not think I could take care of him and provide him with the kind of care he required daily.

"Don't be worried," he said. "I have an attendant who takes care of me in the mornings and evenings."

We talked a lot about it. I prayed and thought about life married to a quadriplegic. I weighed heavily all the negative circumstances and compared them to how much I loved David, how much I loved being with him, and how much he loved and cared for me. I talked with my mom and dad.

A few weeks later I said yes, I would marry him.

David knew I had plans to move to Oklahoma in May of that year to attend Bible College for at least two years, but he gave me a ring anyway. A beautiful golden ring with a ruby as the center stone and three diamonds in a triangular shape on both sides. I wore it with pride and showed it off to everyone.

Before I left, he said, "I guess we just need to trust that God will watch over our relationship while we're apart."

We prayed and left our relationship in God's hands.

After being in Oklahoma for four months, I decided I wanted to marry David. I loved him a lot, wanted to be with him and spend the rest of my life with him. I knew I could continue my Bible-college education in California, so in early August 1990, I moved back.

We married three months later on October 13, 1990, at his home in Saratoga, California. It was a beautiful day — my day. The weather was perfect, warm with a blue sky. The backyard was set up with white chairs facing the house. White blinds provided the backdrop with standing pink and mauve flower pieces marking the place where we said our vows. The day finished smoothly, and we were now Mister and Mrs. David Rodrigues.

Over the next six years we went through the normal adjustments every married couple makes as well as dealing with the stress associated with his physical disability. Our marriage was good, not perfect but strong in spite of the many challenges we faced.

As a newly married couple David and I found unique ways of expressing our physical intimacy; yet our relationship went far deeper than physical attraction. It was about companionship and friendship. We talked openly about everything. Open, honest communication and awareness of meeting each other's needs was a key in our marriage.

I quickly learned what a day in the life of a quadriplegic entailed. Our attendant came into our room every morning at eight o'clock, so I adjusted my waking schedule to get out of bed by seven. I made sure all of my personal clothing was put away for fear that another man would see it.

It took David and his attendant three hours to get ready for the day. His morning routine included a bed bath, shampooing his hair, doing range-of-motion exercises with all his extremities, attaching his leg bag to urinate in, getting dressed, and finally transferring to his wheelchair. Once he was in his chair, he was repositioned, finished dressing, brushed his teeth, shaved, and combed his hair.

While David got ready in the mornings, I spent my time in prayer and daily devotions. Then I cleaned, did laundry, mowed the grass, and performed whatever chores needed done around the house. When David was ready, he came to the kitchen, and we drank a cup of coffee and planned out our day.

David made all the appointments, whatever they were — doctors, automobiles, etc. — and I did the driving. We had a specialized van built for his wheelchair. The inside of the van was empty except for the driver's seat and the bench seat in the back. His electric wheelchair locked into place in the passenger side.

We took Jacob — a special dog we trained to stay at David's side in his wheelchair — with us a lot when we went places. Jacob was a German shepherd and chow mix, medium brown with big brown eyes, about sixty-five pounds. He loved to jump and put his front paws on David's legs, then lay his head down on his lap. The two became inseparable.

One of David's passions included ministering and spending time with people who had physical disabilities. For several months we had a Bible study at our house for disabled people.

David had great compassion for other disabled people. Many looked up to him, saw the inner strength of God's Spirit within him, and wanted it. They wanted to overcome life's challenges as he did. They wanted to find someone to love and marry as he did. They were encouraged by seeing David and me overcome the realities of everyday life with a physical disability.

When David and I went to the hospital for monthly supplies, he liked to visit the spinal-cord ward where he had done much of his rehabilitation. He went into rooms where new spinal-cord injury patients lay in beds, strapped down with metal halos drilled into their skulls to keep their necks stable. He talked with them, prayed with them, and always spoke words of comfort. Seeing David in his wheelchair with a wife by his side gave them hope. It helped them see that their life was not over but taking a different path.

One day we went into the hospital and met a couple whose seventeen-year-old son had broken his neck during a wrestling match and now was a quadriplegic. We went back several times to visit and pray with them. One time when going into this young man's room we saw he had a visitor — the actor who played the role of Radar on the television series "M.A.S.H."

David was excited to meet him and just appalled that I did not know who he was. I never watched "M.A.S.H."

I introduced myself and said it was a pleasure to meet him.

Radar said, "It's okay. When I meet people who don't know me, it keeps me humble."

We took a picture with him, and David gave a brief testimony of God's grace in our lives.

David and I had many fun times together, but we also faced a lot of hard times. His body was prone to severe kidney and bladder infections, and when he got one, it wiped him out. He took so many different antibiotics over the years, his body became immune to them. Frequently the doctors could not find an antibiotic that would kill the infection, and it caused David's pain level to skyrocket.

I felt helpless watching him writhe in pain and not being able to do anything. I prayed for him, but it rarely took away the pain. I think praying gave me the strength to face these situations.

Every few months the infections became so bad, I had to take him to the emergency room. I got him out of bed, into his wheelchair, dressed, and to the hospital. It usually happened at night, so we spent many evenings in the emergency room until 1:00 or 2:00 a.m. or until the doctor found the medication that killed the infection.

Frequently the medication could be given only by a shot directly into David's muscles. I learned to give him the shots, and I did not like it. Feeling the needle puncturing his flesh sent chills through me.

Overall, our life seemed challenging but good. We lived in a home, our marriage was strong, and we loved each other. We set goals of buying our own home, having a family, and traveling more. We attended church, were involved in ministry service as deacons, and I taught Sunday school.

Eventually I did go to Bible college and obtained my bachelor of theology degree. In 1992 I returned to state college, working toward a master's degree in communication sciences and disorders.

During my time in college we lost our attendant care in the evenings, something we never thought would happen. I became David's caretaker at night, performing all the evening routines including putting him in bed. I cleaned the house and completed my homework after he went to bed. My mother, father-in-law, and mother-in-law came over and helped with David's care in the evening when I couldn't get home.

We continued with this routine for the next four years, although it took its toll on all of us. I felt weighed down, because I essentially had three full-time jobs — taking care of David, running the household, and attending graduate school. He spent more time alone, and when I was home, I studied or ran errands.

Frustrated by spending so much time alone, he said things to me like, "You really don't need me around. I'm only pulling you down and holding you back. I don't like you having to take care of me every night."

I acquired my master's degree in June of 1996 and obtained a position in the trauma hospital where I completed my student internship. David was not excited about me working in a hospital, because it meant working longer hours than in the public schools working with children. He saw I enjoyed work but struggled with being alone so much. My work became the topic of many discussions.

After graduation I did not understand the changes that came over the next few months. David wanted me home with him more. He wanted things to be like they were in the beginning of our marriage. I wanted to be active in my field of work, what I studied so long to do. The tension grew, but in my mind I thought things would work out as before. We always prayed, talked about things, and trusted the Lord to help us through whatever challenges we faced. It did not seem different this time.

On Sunday morning, August 11, after David's caretaker finished, we skipped church and went out to breakfast. He was quiet and did not say much. When we arrived home, he asked me to put him in bed.

As we worked, he said to me, "Carolyn, you have a life. I don't have a life. You have your degree now, and you don't need me."

"Stop talking so foolishly. I love you, and I want my life to be with you." Not realizing what his statement really meant, I added, "Oh, David, what would I do without you? What would I do without my David?"

He responded in an unnerving solemn tone, "You will go on with God."

The following morning, August 12, 1996, after his caretaker left, David committed suicide. I often wonder why he did that to himself and to me. I walked through the ensuing journey of grief and finally found rest for my soul.

The subsequent chapters address the different seasons of grief a suicide survivor often confronts, with examples taken from my journal writings. At the end of the book I give suggestions for counselors, ministers, and family members of suicide survivors.

"It is because of the potential power of grief that we need people outside us to help us get a sense of perspective, and to judge what kind of help we need."[2]

These are my thoughts in painful honesty as I walked through a life-transforming journey during the aftermath of David's suicide.

Chapter Three

Help In Times Of Mourning

Be merciful to me, Lord, for I am faint
O Lord, heal me, for my bones are In agony.
My soul is in anguish. How long, O Lord, how long?
— Psalm 6:2-3

I really think I'm going crazy sometimes!
So many things just run through my head.
Why didn't I tell him I loved him that morning? Neither of us ever let me leave the house
without saying, "I love you," to one another,
even when we had an argument.

Today was a numb day for me. I still have
much pain within. Is it normal to feel afraid
after someone close has died? Sometimes it
feels as though it's becoming worse rather
than better.

I have been crying more frequently, and
when I cry, it feels as if it hurts worse than in
the beginning. Is that part of the healing pro-

cess? The process of a broken heart healing is a strange one. I wonder if one's heart is ever really completely healed?

Journal Entry,
August 30, 1996

Mourning, for me, was an intense chaotic wilderness of grief, shock, and disbelief that my husband committed suicide and I found him dead. It continues over many months and years. The only way I can describe mourning after a suicide is that it is an "emotional war." Pain, anger, sadness, confusion, tears, and loneliness became my constant companions.

Thoughts bombarded my mind like a continual spray of bullets fired by a machine gun.

Why did he do it? What could I have done to prevent it? What am I going to do now? Where is God? Is David in Heaven? Where am I going to live?

I had absence of peace in my soul.

After the funeral I felt lost. My husband now gone, I did not know what to do with myself. The house and David's wheelchair sat empty. I felt pain as never before, similar to someone taking a knife, thrusting it deep into my gut, and turning without stopping. It was agonizing.

My confusion and disorientation lasted for several months. My conversations with people had no coherence, and I jumped from topic to topic, unable to maintain my train of thought.

Frequently I thought, *What am I doing, and how did I get here?*

I spent hours every day crying. I wandered aimlessly day in and day out, hoping to find peace. My emotions were uncontrollable. One fleeting thought of David or a visual memory of finding him, and I burst into tears or became angry. My emotions raged so intensely and sporadically, I could not sense God's presence. I yelled out to Him for peace; only silence returned. It was a time of breaking down and utter destruction of my life as I knew it.

> How did I ever get to this moment in my life? I never dreamed that my life would be shaken to the very foundation of my existence at the ripe old age of twenty-nine. My husband is dead from suicide. The storm is raging within me, but somehow — I don't know how — I keep going.
>
> Journal Entry,
> August 25, 1996

The change in my life was so sudden and traumatic, it paralyzed me emotionally, mentally, spiritually, and physically. The haunting images of finding David dead played over and over in my mind. My reasoning, judgment, memory, and attention were poor from my emotional state.

Physically, although exhausted, I was unable to sleep. I paced through my kitchen and family room, crying and watching the clock as the minutes and hours passed. Finally, I would fall asleep on the couch in the early-morning hours.

My hunger disappeared. I lost more than twenty-five pounds. I had headaches and often did not have the energy to get up in the mornings.

> I'm feeling very exhausted tonight, I was exhausted all day. I'm not really feeling well physically. I feel like everything has caught up with me. All I want to do is sleep or just lie on my bed. I'm so tired and drained. I try to sleep, but I can't. My body and my mind feel as though they've been through World War III!
>
> Journal Entry,
> September 12, 1996

During the first year of mourning I became so depressed and sad, I think it made people want to avoid me, probably from fear of not knowing what to do or say. I said I did not care, but deep down I longed for someone to talk with me. I wanted to talk about David's death, his suicide, but was unable to find anyone who did not change the subject when I brought up his name in conversation.

One afternoon I came across a poem that I received through a flyer in the mail. It clearly captures what it was like when I needed others to acknowledge David's death and talk to me about his suicide — but they didn't.

The Elephant in the Room
by Terry Kettering

There's an elephant in the room.

It is large and squatting, so it is hard to get around it.
Yet we squeeze by with, "How are you?"
And, "I'm fine"...
And a thousand other forms of trivial chatter.
We talk about the weather.
We talk about work.
We talk about everything else -
Except the elephant in the room.

There's an elephant in the room.
We all know it is there.
We are thinking about the elephant as we talk together.
It is constantly on our minds.
For, you see, it is a very big elephant.
It has hurt us all.
But we do not talk about the elephant in the room.
Oh, please, say her name
Oh, please, say "Barbara" again.

Oh, please, let's talk about the elephant in the room.
For if we talk about her death,
Perhaps we can talk about her life?
Can I say "Barbara" to you and not have you look away?
For if I cannot, then you are leaving me
Alone...
In a room...
With an elephant.

*Reprinted with permission from Bereavement Publishing, Inc.
(888-604-4673/www.bereavementresources.com)*

I talked about David with Anita, my friend and colleague at the time. I paged her at work so much, she did not know what to do. She did not want to tell me to stop calling, because she knew I was a mess emotionally. She finally made a phone call — unknown to me — to Hospice of the Valley, where I could get professional grief counseling. She got in touch with a social worker and crisis counselor, Corrie Marcellino, who told Anita I had to call and make the appointment.

At first, when Anita told me she thought I needed more help in dealing with David's suicide and that she had called Corrie, I was defensive.

I thought, *Why do I want to talk to some stranger about my life and my husband's suicide. What can she do to help me?*

I thought about it for a few days.

One day when I paged Anita three or four times and she did not respond, I realized I really did need professional help. I finally worked up the courage to call Corrie. While at work, I wrote down a script of what to say so I would not forget anything.

I picked up the phone. My heart was pounding, and I was sweating.

When I asked for Corrie, the secretary said she was not available at the time, but if I left my number, she would get back with me later.

I left my pager number and thought, *Whew! That's over.*

I went about my day in the hospital and received a page while walking down the hallway on one of the medical floors upstairs. I looked at my pager and did not recognize the number at first. Then it dawned on me that it was Corrie.

Oh, no! I thought, *I don't have my script with me. What am I going to say to her?*

I stopped in the hallway where there was a telephone and not many people around, and I called her. She had a pleasant and caring voice on the telephone.

"What's happening?" she said.

"Um...my husband committed suicide," I responded, "and I'm having a hard time dealing with it."

A lump formed in my throat, and my vision blurred from the tears welling up in my eyes. My voice began quivering. I was on the verge of crying.

She told me, "I think it would be very helpful if we met and talked for a while."

She said some other things that I don't recall, but I remember how comfortable she made me feel on the telephone. That was what gave me the courage to make an appointment with her.

It was the best decision I ever made. I connected with someone who understood what I was experiencing. She provided insight and wisdom about grief after suicide and validated all of my emotions — guilt, anger, depression, sadness, doubt, and fear. God worked instrumentally through Corrie to help me face the reality of David's suicide. With her help I gained the courage to look at what had happened, confront my own fears, and eventually arrive in a place of acceptance. She walked me through to complete healing and was an integral part in every season of my grief.

Six months after David's suicide, I began having flashbacks of the day I found him dead and the day of the funeral. Scenes from those times flashed before my eyes everywhere I went. Walking down the hallway, going to the supermarket, driving down the road, the flashbacks persisted. I could not control my emotions.

I called Corrie and told her what was happening. She asked if I would come in earlier than our next appointment. A few days passed before I could get in to see her, but she stayed in close contact with me, calling daily to make sure I was all right.

I told her, "I think I'm going crazy, and I don't want to live like this."

It frightened me. I thought I was having a nervous breakdown.

When I finally saw Corrie, I explained to her again about the flashbacks. I kept seeing David's face; his cold, stiff body; the black body bag; the casket at the cemetery; hundreds of eyes staring at me.

"Close your eyes," she said, "and relax."

She took me through the day I found David and the day of the funeral. I relived the events, but this time I allowed myself to experience the feelings and emotions. I had pushed down so much to keep myself together, I had not allowed myself to experience them before.

As Corrie walked me through the day I found him, she said, "Remember I'm here, and you're safe. Tell me everything you're thinking and what you're feeling."

For the first time I felt sheer terror.

I cried uncontrollably. "Oh, my God! Oh, my God! What did I do to you?"

As I cried, I felt the gut-wrenching tears and pain coming from deep inside.

"He's dead," I said.

"Yes, he's dead," she responded.

"He killed himself."

"Yes, he did."

"He knew I would find him. Why did he let me find him?"

"Yes, he knew you would find him."

"Oh, he looks so awful. Look at him. Look over there. The closet is open, and his medication tray is pulled out. Look, his Bible is open to the book of Proverbs. The stereo is on with worship music playing. He must have been in so much pain, Corrie."

"Yes, he must have been in a lot of pain."

We continued, and I experienced the entire evening and the day of the funeral.

Corrie asked, "What do you see at the cemetery?"

"I'm walking up the path. There are a lot of trees around. The grass is deep green. I can see the plot where it's been dug out for his casket. Flowers are everywhere. I'm sitting down in the front row. The sun is beating down on me. My pastor is talking in slow motion. I feel a hundred pairs of eyes staring at me. I see his casket right in front of me with the swirling detail designs in the handles. There's the hole. He's really going down there. I don't want him to go down there. If he goes down there, he'll never come back."

"That's right. He's not coming back."

"Corrie, he's really dead!"

"Yes, Carolyn, he's really dead."

I ended up sitting on the floor in front of Corrie's chair, holding my knees together with my arms and my head down. She held me as I wept bitter and painful tears.

"I'm here," she said. "You're not alone anymore. You're safe."

I placed what little trust I had left in Corrie, and she gave me a sense of security and safety. She walked me through the most painful and heart-rending moments I've ever had to face. I met with her once a week for over a year, then once every two weeks, then once a month until we agreed I could go on without seeing her any longer. She made herself available to me if I needed to talk.

When I did stop counseling, I was downhearted. I felt as if something more was being taken from me. I shared my life, my pain, my dreams, and my triumphs with Corrie for more than two years, and I felt nervous about walking on alone.

She affirmed the new strength that developed within me and supported me during my transition into walking on my own two feet. I know if I had not had her in my life and gone to grief counseling, I would not be here. She became a lighthouse for me in the middle of my sinking life. I believe God providentially placed her in my life. I consider her my angel on earth.

During the first several months of mourning it was hard reaching out to others and calling people. I rarely returned phone calls. I felt as though I could not call anyone. I felt awkward telling someone other than Corrie or Anita that I was having a hard day.

One of the things that bothered me most during these months was when people said to me, "Call if you need anything."

I wanted to scream at them, "I won't call! Just call me!"

> Everybody says don't be afraid to call. Call if you need to talk. Call if you need anything. I won't call. I don't have the ability to call anyone. I can't bring myself to do it. Why don't they just call me?
>
> Journal Entry,
> September 7, 1996

When I did talk to others, especially friends and people within my church, one of the most helpful things they did was to accept my emotional state. They did not try to change the way I felt. Many people were shocked by the things that came bursting out of my mouth. I surprised *myself*. They did not say anything but just listened. It was what I needed at the time.

> I'm so angry tonight! I felt like such a bitch all day long. I called a friend of mine, and she got an ear full of my anger. It just came bursting out! Thank God she just listened and understood.
>
> I apologized to her, but in her gentle response to my anger she said, "You have a right to be angry. It's okay."

35

I'm angry, and I hate David right now
for putting me in this situation! I love him
and I hate him at the same time. Does that
make sense?

Journal Entry,
September 24, 1996

My thoughts appalled me sometimes, and I found
myself thinking about being in a position of leadership
at church. I felt I was not portraying "Christian character"; in reality I portrayed human grief after suicide.

Over time I sensed people at church also had a
hard time dealing with David's suicide.

Coming from a Christian perspective, thoughts and
questions consumed me such as, *Where did David go? Is he
with Jesus?*

It took more than two years to resolve this huge
struggle and come to peace with it. During those years
people asked me if I thought David was in hell for committing suicide, or they insinuated that he was in hell. I
struggled so much with the issue already, I did not need
those questions asked. They triggered anger not only at
the person asking, but also at God.

People say such stupid things sometimes!
It's so hurtful when people say stupid things
to you. I know they don't understand. People
really don't have a clue of how to bring into
balance suicide and God. I don't either, but
I probably have a little bit more of an understanding than most. People don't look at me

in the eyes when I talk about David's suicide. They even sometimes insinuate that he's
gone to hell! I can't believe it!
Journal Entry,
January 10, 1997

In people's zealous attempts to make things better, some wanted to pray for me. The first few times I let others pray for me, I had them tell me what God wanted me to do. It unnerved me when others told me that God wanted me to do all of these things.

I could not sense God's presence at the time, and I was still angry at Him. I did not want a word from a God at Whom I was angry. I did not want to read about or pray to a God Whom I perceived allowed my husband to kill himself. I could not take care of myself emotionally and get through a whole day at work, much less try to read my Bible.

After that I became selective about who I would let pray for me. Corrie helped me learn how to take things in stride and recognize it was in people's lack of knowledge about grief and their honest desire to help that they said those things.

Working with Corrie and moving through the time of mourning, I realized that by talking about David and his suicide, inner healing came. I had many questions that neither Corrie nor my pastors could answer. I did not want answers. I just needed someone to listen. I did not need to be preached to or hear religious clichés. I needed people to be there, give me a hug when I needed it, and reassure me God had not left, that I would make it.

Over time I integrated David's death. It no longer consumed me. I came to a place where I did not need to talk about him all the time, and I began to focus on my own life. I no longer obsessed about finding out why he killed himself. I left it in God's hands and trusted that He knew why, even if I did not.

Ultimately I came to the place where I accepted that, *The secret things belong to the Lord our God, but the things revealed belong to us* (Deut. 29:29). I recognized that, while working through my grief and mourning, I had to let go of my obsession about finding out why.

There remained much unfulfilled and unfinished in our lives, and I wanted him back. No amount of prayer, desire, or crying could bring him back. No number of words could change my circumstances. I had to work through the grief.

With Corrie's help, support from close friends, and my pastors, I was able to mourn, validate, and experience my emotions. All these things allowed healing to take place and the ashes of my grief to eventually dissipate.

As I have reflected back on my moments of truth and honesty in acknowledging my husband's suicide, I have realized it has been a time of painful honesty for those around me as well. I have realized that others had difficulty accepting David's death by suicide. A book I read, *No Time to Say Good-bye,* says that suicide is not a topic that is openly discussed. It is a stain that blemishes the illusion of normalcy.

Could it be that I held an "illusion of Christian normalcy?" The normalcy being that because I have God in my life, I am somehow exempt from tragic circumstances coming into my life — most of all suicide? What I have perceived as the silence of God, the desperately dark and lonely times of mourning, has driven me into a deeper search for God.

Journal Entry,
February 8, 1998

Chapter Four

Times Of Guilt And Depression

Turn, O Lord, and deliver me;
I am worn out from groaning;
All night long I flood my bed with weeping
And drench my couch with tears.
My eyes grow weak with sorrow;
They fail because of all my foes.
— Psalm 6:6-7

I'll never ever forget the day I found him dead. The way he looked, the feelings of guilt that rushed over me like an angry tidal wave. "Oh my God, what did I do to you? What did I do to make you do this?" The overwhelming feeling of hopelessness that must have seized his heart — the way I feel right now — I wasn't there to help him. I wasn't there for him.

Journal Entry,
August 28, 1996

Guilt is the defining emotion that set my grief apart from normal grief after loss. My guilt and depression lasted for more than two years. Around holidays or the anniversary dates of our wedding and his suicide, the depression always rolled in and settled like fog.

I went through cycles of asking myself what I could have done to prevent him from committing suicide.

I continually asked, *What if...?*

What if I had prayed more? What if I had tried to talk to him more? What if I had called someone from the church and had them come over to talk with David? What if I had done this or that?

These questions plagued and tormented my mind for the first two years. I felt guilty because of the times I treated him badly or we had an argument. I thought about all the nasty things I ever said to him and felt guilty. I felt I should have been there for him more. The guilt consumed me so much, I plunged into deep periods of depression.

> For weeks now I've been depressed. I've never experienced depression and low points in my life like this before. It feels like no one cares, but to be honest about it, I don't care either. I haven't cared for several weeks now. I don't know if it's depression or maybe I've developed some attitude. I don't know.
>
> The scary thing is, I'm not one who gets depressed easily, and being in this place I feel as though I spiral downward and it's difficult to get back up. How do I make it

through when it hurts so deeply? I don't know what's important to care about. I cared about something or someone, I poured my life into my marriage — all of me. I gave because I cared so much. Look where it ended up! Is it any wonder that I fail to want to care about anything?

Journal Entry,
February 10, 1997

My depression began as the shock and numbness wore off. I wanted to withdraw from people and keep myself isolated.

Corrie was the only one I talked to. I leaned on her, and she helped me understand my depression and overall mental state. She listened to what I said, she loved me, and she encouraged me. She spoke into my life with a gentle, bold confidence and helped me see that ultimately I could not have done anything to prevent his suicide. I probably could have prevented it for a day, maybe two, but when a person has decided to complete the act of suicide, there is little anyone can do. It comes down to human freewill and choice.

During this time people around me in church, at work, and my family said, "This is not your fault. You didn't do anything to make him commit suicide. Don't take the blame."

It's easy to tell a suicide survivor, "Don't take the blame. It's not your fault," but it was difficult not to take the blame. I loved him. I took care of him. He took care of me. We shared all of our intimate moments together.

We shared each other's dreams and visions. I would have done anything for him.

After his suicide, I realized David did not share everything with me as he said he did. I felt as if he did not trust me enough to share his tormenting thoughts with me. He did not let me into part of his life. I felt betrayed. It facilitated guilt. I felt I did something to keep him from fully trusting me.

In my struggle with guilt, thinking I could have done something to prevent David's suicide, Corrie said something that released me from the torment in my mind.

She said, "If God didn't do anything to prevent David from committing suicide, because of David's free will, what makes you think you could have done any more to stop him from killing himself? You're giving yourself a lot of power, even above God, if you think you could have stopped him!"

Her words startled me. It made me realize I really did not have any say or control over another human being's choice to take his own life — although it is painful to think about, given how much I loved him. When I accepted this, it brought freedom to my mind and released much of the guilt that crushed me. The questions eventually dissipated as I resolved his suicide in my heart.

During my times of depression I battled with thoughts of suicide myself. It scared me. It made sense to me at times. I wanted it at times.

When I went through these periods, I talked with Corrie a lot in my sessions and on the telephone. She stayed close to me during such times. She must have been a little nervous herself. Whenever I gave hints of thinking about suicide, she immediately brought it out in the open, and we talked about it. She validated how overwhelmed I felt and how much pain I was in.

Often I did not want to live through another minute.

A terrible day...I seem to crash so easily these days! I woke up this morning and just felt so down and sadness engulfed my heart. I cried all day today. I eventually cried myself to sleep for a few hours. I am so lonely right now.

How do I find God when I'm in such a place? Why can't I feel His presence? Why don't I have any hope for the future? It's very hard to continue on in life when you have no vision, no goals for the future, when you don't see anything ahead of you. All I see are more days of sadness, crying and hopelessness. Is it any wonder that if David was feeling this way he killed himself?

I have thoughts of suicide myself lately. Is it crazy for me to be having thoughts of suicide? Why am I having these thoughts? What if I decided to kill myself? To check out on life. I have everything I would need to do it right here in my apartment. What would happen? I certainly would end all the pain that I'm going through right now, all that I would have to go through in the future.

The bad part is that I would hurt so many people who are left behind — Corrie, my immediate family, my best friends, and my church family — all of whom are very special to me. I don't think I could do it for that very reason. I couldn't put anyone else through the same hell that I have had to go through this past year.

Journal Entry
August 31, 1997

Talking with Corrie about my thoughts of suicide dismantled the power those thoughts held over me. She helped me realize those feelings were only temporary and that I did have a future.

Corrie and I talked at length about depression, what it was, and how to manage it. At one point she recommended I take antidepressant medication. I did not want to because David had overdosed on drugs.

Then she recommended I become involved in extracurricular activities. We talked about me going to a friend's house or out to dinner with people even when I did not feel like it. I forced myself to do these things. It was hard, because I did not want to be out. I wanted to be home on my couch.

Many times when I was alone or isolated from other people for prolonged periods I became depressed. It made me feel as though I could not make it any further.

I can't do it anymore! I'm losing the battle that's warring in my soul. It hurts so much inside.

I can hardly bear the thought of David never being here again. I don't want him to be gone. I want him with me. I want to hear his voice one more time.

It's so painful, so lonely, and no one here to comfort the agony and despair in my soul. I want to be held, and there's no one to hold me. No one knows the thousands of tears I've cried. Does anyone really care in this dark night in my life?

Journal Entry,
May 22, 1997

My emotions were in such a state of turmoil, I was unable to sense God's presence, and I became spiritually apathetic. I was angry at God. I felt guilty not wanting to read my Bible, pray, or even go to church. It made me more depressed when I did not sense anything spiritual about myself.

I struggled thinking about the head knowledge I had of God — and it did not seem to be relevant anymore.

I cried all morning long. I cried out to God, because I need Him to give me the desire to read my Bible again. I don't have any desire to pick it up. Once in a while I pick it up and read a Psalm or Proverb, but that's about it. I read one of the gospels a few weeks ago, and my thoughts were, *I need*

God's word to be relevant to my life and my life's circumstances. How can I read the Bible and really be able to relate it to my life and apply it to my circumstances?

I need God so desperately but am unable to bring myself to do anything to find Him during this very dark night of my soul.

Journal Entry,
February 7, 1997

The dawning of a new day came slowly like the sunrise. The dark night of my soul, guilt and depression, receded over time. The way it receded is hard to put into words, but it was an event of God's Spirit. It was supernatural, and it happened over time.

Being in church, in the presence of God, even when I could not feel His presence, brought healing to my wounded soul and spirit. It was also an act of my will. I had to get out and do things and be with other people.

Corrie continued challenging me to change my way of thinking. I learned from going through the periods of depression that if I kept myself isolated, I developed negative thoughts. I have realized that I will probably continue to experience periodic times of depression, but now I have strategies to deal with those times. I have friends I can call — and instead of waiting on others to call me, I have learned to call them.

I began to turn my focus of attention away from myself. I tried to be alert and aware of not allowing myself to dwell on negative, self-condemning thoughts.

I began to reach out to others in need — not necessarily grieving people, but others who needed help in general. When my focus of how I believed others should be helping me was transformed into how I could help others through what God was doing in my own life, the depression faded. I realized I became a walking, living epistle of God's grace and faithfulness. I reached out to others whom I sensed needed a friend, and there came a new ease with which I was able to listen to others. I accepted them where they were in life and loved them for who they were.

As I continued to focus outwardly and reach out to others with God's love and compassion, I knew I had found what the essence of Christianity is all about. God loved us when we were unlovable. He wanted us back in relationship with Him, so He gave His life for us. He accepts us just as we are.

I learned it should not be any different in our relationship with others. It was through my season of guilt and depression that the Lord taught me how to change my thinking. When I acted on those changes, it helped bring me through to the other side. Hope and the light of God permeated the dark night of my soul. Through the events in everyday life my depression gave way to new joy in my heart.

I smiled and laughed today as I watched my niece and nephews play. I felt my heart smile as my nephew gave me a big bear hug! It really is okay to have joy and laughter in my life again. It feels good to laugh. It feels good to smile inside. Laughter is good medicine for my soul.

Journal Entry,
May 16, 1999

Chapter Five

Times Of Anger
And Pain

My heart is in anguish within me;
the terrors of death assail me.
Fear and trembling have beset me;
Horror has overwhelmed me.
I said, "Oh, that I had the wings of a
Dove! I would fly away and be at rest-
I would flee far away and stay in the
Desert; I would hurry to my place of shelter,
Far from the tempest and storm."
— Psalm 55:4-8

Emotionally, I'm a mess! I cried all day, but as the day went on, I became irritated and frustrated at everyone and everything. The bottom line was that I was downright bitchy to people around me. I felt bad about it later and apologized to one of my co-workers whom I yelled at.

I went to see Corrie, and she seems to think it's a lot of anger within me that needs to come out in a healthier manner! I know I'm angry. I just have a hard time letting it out. Corrie wants me to list some things I'm angry about, so here goes:

I'm angry that I'm alone and David made that decision for me. I'm angry that he killed himself. I'm mad because I've been forced to do all these things and make decisions I haven't wanted to make, and I'm mad that I even have to go through all this grieving!

Journal Entry,
January 15, 1997

In the beginning of grief, "There is no comfort. Absence becomes the only presence. Too much has been left unsaid, unfinished, unfulfilled. There is so much you wanted to share. You feel an overpowering desire to be reunited with your loved one. You want to undo this ruthless separation."[1]

Unable to be comforted, I spent hours crying in screams of rage. Some days so much anger built up inside me, I paced through my house like a caged animal. I could not release the anger for fear I would lose control if I let it out. I was angry at David, at God, and at the world around me. I often snapped at people who were trying to talk to me. I had little patience for anything.

I'm so angry right now, I just feel sick inside! I'm really alone. I don't have anyone to talk to. Hell, they couldn't do anything anyway! God, all I can do is lie here screaming and crying! Where do I go? What do I do? The agony and despair in my soul is so intense!

Journal Entry,
September 1, 1996

Frequently after the suicide of a loved one, "You become annoyed at anyone connected with the event of death. You reject the overtures of your friends. How dare they talk of your future when you know life holds nothing for you? You are infuriated with your loved one for leaving you. Your anger should be recognized, not suppressed. Angry thoughts and feelings help to express frustrations."[2]

I did become annoyed at everyone in my life. I rejected many of my friends. My future looked bleak and empty. In the beginning the only way I could release my anger was through tears.

The first time I ever let myself feel and express my anger was after a counseling session with Corrie. She recognized my difficulty in dealing with my anger. She suggested when I felt angry, taking a black crayon and scribbling on a piece of paper. I thought it rather silly at first, but I tried it. I had to try something. My anger consumed me.

I went home, and the following day I remember feeling the anger beginning to well up inside. Standing in my empty bedroom, I looked around and felt the power of death and anger surrounding me. I knelt on the floor and began scratching on a piece of paper with a black crayon. I scribbled so hard, the crayon broke, and I threw it at the wall.

I screamed out, "No!"

My rage poured out as I knelt there in the middle of my bedroom and screamed with agonizing tears as loudly as I could.

During my next session I told Corrie what happened. I told her the scribbling part did not work, because the crayon broke.

When she asked me what happened next, I told her, and she said, "Then it did work."

I allowed myself the freedom to cry, but Corrie reminded me that tears were not a sign of weakness. They were a means of healing.

My pain was so great at times, I thought I could not survive another moment. I often wondered how I made it through each day.

My heart is in tremendous pain — pain that doesn't have words to even describe it. It feels as though someone is tearing me apart from the inside out. It hurts so much to think about the amount of pain that David had deep within his soul. The anguish that must have been present, not allowing him to see any hope for the future — the way I feel right now. It hurts so deeply when I cry. The loneliness is intense, the grief and pain intolerable sometimes.

The whole cycle that I go through day in and day out — will it ever end? Is there ever an end to grief? Is there ever an end to the pain I feel inside that day after day I have to push down in order to move through the day?

Journal Entry,
January 30, 1997

I clearly remember a day going into Corrie's office when immediately she looked at me and asked, "What's going on?"

I sank down in the corner, covered my head, and said, "I can't do this anymore. It hurts too much, and I don't want to do this any longer. I'm not going to make it."

I will never forget the way she responded. She hugged me and spoke to me with such gentleness, telling me that I *would* make it.

"You've made it this far," she said. "You'll make it the rest of the way. I'll walk with you the rest of the way."

I sobbed in her embrace. I needed to be held at that moment. I needed the assurance that I could make it. I needed comfort, and I allowed Corrie to comfort me. My choice in allowing someone to comfort me was a key to my healing. Corrie's touch in the form of a hug and an embrace brought a powerful sense of love, safety, peace, and reassurance. It brought the glimmer of hope I needed to continue.

Allowing my anger to be released, I realized it had the potential of turning into bitterness and unforgiveness.

It had the potential of becoming a great wall for stopping my healing if I did not deal with it.

About two years after David's death I sensed the need to confront my unforgivenenss toward David, God, and myself. It was a difficult step of faith to take.

I don't fully understand how it happened, but I continually made a choice to say out loud, "I forgive you David for taking your life and hurting me so deeply."

If I found myself with angry thoughts, I expressed them aloud to God. I told God I was angry with Him, and I forgave God as well. God did not need me to say I forgave Him, but I did. I was angry at God for letting David kill himself and not doing anything to stop it. I told God everything I thought. I am thankful for God's unconditional love and acceptance.

I read in a story somewhere about a man whose son died tragically at a young age, and the man struggled with forgiving God. He asked, "Where was God when my son died?"

Someone responded to him, "The same place He was when *His* son died."

This story pierced me deeply. I realized for the first time that we all live in a fallen, sinful world, and tragic circumstances are a part of life. God is still God, and He has given us His love through redemption, grace, and mercy to walk through the tragedies of life. We overcome them through the power of Christ's completed work on the cross.

This was a pathway I had to walk down if I expected to be completely healed and have my life restored. I continually made the choice to forgive myself as well.

Today is the second anniversary of David's death. I went to the cemetery, sat down in front of his grave, and began talking to him. I expressed my love for him and how much I missed him. I told him how far God had brought me after the horrible day that I had found him. I told him I was angry and hated him sometimes for killing himself, but I was finally able to forgive him and to forgive myself. I felt as though he was really there in spirit, listening to every word I was saying.

I stayed for a few hours. I didn't cry. I just sat there and talked to him. When I finally did decide to leave, I felt released from much of the grief that had covered me for so long. I felt freedom within my soul to really move on with my life.

It didn't take away the fact that there are still moments when I think about him and cry because I miss him. When those moments come, it's no longer a stirring of anger but of love that wells up within me and says, "I loved you, David. I will always love you. You will always hold a very special place in my heart."

Journal Entry,
August 12, 1998

It is a living example of the power of forgiveness, which provided a means of releasing the deep pain that accompanied my anger. As another way of releasing my pain and anger, I wrote a letter to David, letting him know my thoughts and how deeply he had hurt me.

December 8, 1996

Dear David,

I'm writing this letter to you because I have a lot of things I need to say to you and because I miss you very much. You see, when you were here, I could sit and talk to you about how I was feeling. You were always good about just listening, but then you always took it one step further — you prayed for me.

There was something about having my husband, my protector, always there if I felt like my soul was struggling. Whether it was sadness, low self-esteem, anger, or frustration, you were always there as my covering to pray for me. I always had peace after you prayed for me. I think sometimes I relied so much on your faith that I neglected to put my own faith into action. I feel as if I don't have any faith right now. I feel as though everything about me, who I was, has just been stripped off layer by layer, and now I really don't know who this person is that remains. I miss you so much.

Right now I wish I could just see your
face, look into your beautiful green eyes, and
tell you that your life truly counted for God.
I want to tell you that the Lord used you in
a powerful way to touch the lives of many
people. You always had an ability to reach
beyond the circumstances of our lives, your
own pain, and allow God to minister His
love, grace, and peace through you to others. What happened?

I think about you at the moment you
killed yourself. I think about the tremendous
amount of pain you must have been in at
that moment. The thoughts are like arrows
that shoot right through my heart. It's so overwhelming for me when I think about these
things that I become paralyzed, frozen, and
I don't know what to do. It makes me think
about God, when His only son Jesus gave
His life so that we could live eternally in
Heaven — the amount of pain He went
through as His only Son was dying on the
cross for our sins so that we could have and
experience eternal life with Him.

I'm sorry to say that since you committed suicide, my entire life, the very foundation has been shaken. I haven't been a godly
example to people around me, but you know
what? My friends have loved me anyway. I
know that in spite of myself, God has loved
me and carried me through this most

devastating time in my life. Although I don't feel like reading my Bible or praying, God loves me just as I am.

David, I don't know if I'll make it. I so desperately need God to touch me and heal the brokenness inside. When I found you dead in your wheelchair, your eyes just staring through me, your face sickly looking, your body cold and stiff — I lost something within me. It shook me to the very core. I was very scared; I still am. My confidence in life just drained out of me. My confidence in my ability to teach, in my ability at work was wiped out. It's been a terrible time trying to regain my confidence that God has not left me as well and that I'm really going to make it.

In this dark night of my soul, in the valley of the shadow of death, it's so hard to sense God's presence, to see any light. Maybe you can just pray for me one more time and ask God to help me. I can't go on without God. What is life without Jesus? Nothing — black, obsolete, no hope for the future. I need Him to bring hope and joy back into my heart.

David, I'm so very sorry that we didn't have the opportunity to fulfill all the dreams and visions we held in our hearts. Maybe one day I'll find the ability to dream and hope again. I miss talking to you, I miss you holding me, I miss you praying for me, I miss kissing you, and I miss seeing your smiling face.

I want you to know that I'm going to grief counseling, because I'm having such a hard time dealing with your suicide. Some days I think I'm going to make it; other days I don't think I'll make it another minute. I often wonder why you didn't leave me a note or anything at all. You hurt me deeply. Do you see me now? Do you see the pain and anguish that just rage through my soul day after day? Do you really think I can go on with God?

Store this letter in heaven with you.

With all my love forever —
Carolyn

Writing this letter to David allowed me to share my thoughts with him in a tangible way and brought a release of inner healing to my wounded soul. It did not happen overnight; it took time. Facing the pain of the reality of my husband's suicide allowed me to move on with my life.

Earl Grollman, in his book *Living When a Loved One Has Died*, talks about reality in this manner. "Your loved one has not 'gone away on a long journey,' 'passed on,' 'departed,' 'passed away,' 'expired.' Your loved one is dead. What is — what cannot be changed — must be accepted. Even though it may be the most difficult thing you have ever done, you must face reality. The funeral is over. The flowers have withered. Now the loss becomes real. Your loved one is dead."[3]

The pain of suicide — when I came face to face with my pain, it was excruciating. Each time I faced it, I became more aware I needed a redeemer, I needed a healer. Each time I faced the pain and allowed myself to experience it, healing came just a little bit more. The pain and anger receded over time as I chose to forgive David, God, and myself. It happened without my awareness, and only God was able to redeem me from my place of darkness.

> The acuteness, the sharpness, the feeling of just hurting isn't as strong as it was before. I can't even begin to recollect when it began to diminish. I just happened to come upon the realization one day that the pain wasn't as intense. I think that was the importance of having people walking closely to me, encouraging me to continue on and reminding me that the enormity of the pain would lessen over time. I didn't think the pain would ever lessen, but it did!
>
> Journal Entry,
> July 29, 1997

As Thomas C. Hart wrote: "Oh, God, give me the courage to change the things I can change, the serenity to accept that which I cannot change, and the wisdom to distinguish between the two." *(Prayer of St. Francis)*

Chapter Six

Has God Abandoned Me?

My God, my God, why have you forsaken me?
Why are you so far from saving me,
So far from the words of my groaning?
Oh, my God, I cry out by day, but you do not
Answer, by night, and am not silent.
— Psalm 22:1-2

How did I ever get to this moment in
my life? God is not here right now. I feel far
away — God is far away. God, where are
you? God, do you see me now? Are you really there? I need God, and He is nowhere
to be found. My soul is screaming out for
His peace and comfort — but He's not here.
Journal Entry,
September 17, 1996

The war within my soul was a sense of God aban-
doning me. My battle with feeling as though I lost my

faith was a huge part of the aftermath of my husband's suicide. I was convinced that just as David had abandoned me, God had left me as well. I went through the beginning seasons of my grief continually asking where God was. My anger raged, and I hated God at times for the silence of heaven during my most intense hour of need.

I asked Him, "Why didn't You stop him? How could David have committed suicide with his Bible open and praise and worship music playing? It doesn't make sense to me."

God, all knowing, all-powerful...why didn't God let me know in some way or somehow warn me?

I woke up every morning with an ache inside — desperately angry at God, desperately begging God for His presence, desperately asking for help to find peace.

> Struggling — I feel as though I'm not going make it. I'm struggling so much with my life right now. Looking into the unknown. Struggling with my faith. I really don't know what faith is anymore. I keep going to church, putting on my face, and pretending I really do still believe and that I have faith. It's not working inside. My soul is being torn apart inside! A battle is raging inside!
>
> I don't want David to be gone — I want him back. I hate You, God, for not doing anything to stop him from killing himself! I

hate You for not doing anything right now!
Why are You silent? Stop the silence!

Journal Entry,
May 5, 1997

Corrie and I spent countless hours talking about my sense of God leaving me. We talked more about this issue than anything.

I was so sure God had abandoned me that in one of my sessions, Corrie asked if I was willing to have the chaplain come in and talk with me. I said yes. He came in, sat down, and Corrie explained to him what happened and why I was there for counseling.

As soon as he sat down, I looked at him. I saw peace and the presence of God surrounding him. I wanted it.

I burst into tears and told him, "I have to find God. I can't find him anywhere. I need God. I can't go on without God."

I was desperate, and he sensed it.

In his gracious response he said, "Carolyn, first let me tell you that your desire for God is bouncing off these walls."

He went on without preaching to me but feeding me the Word of God. He shared many scripture passages about God saying He would never leave us nor forsake us in our time of need.

I was able to receive God's word from him, because he didn't give me religious clichés such as, "Well, David is in Heaven now. He's in a better place. He's walking now. He no longer has to suffer in his wheelchair. Praise God that he is with the Lord now," and the list goes on.

My husband was dead, and I did not want to hear anything about praising God at the time. I was angry at God. I knew all of those things, but the reality was that I was hurting and in pain from the loss of my husband. The chaplain did not tell me what God wanted me to do, but simply shared with compassion the truth of God's Word in normal everyday language.

Sitting there crying and asking him where God was, I looked over at Corrie as she held my hand. Tears streamed down her face. For the first and only time she observed the session from the outside — able to see, feel, and experience the desperate pain I felt.

It is hard to make sense of my struggle with faith and God. There is so much that doesn't make sense to a suicide survivor.

I felt shame before God and before the world. I believed God thought it was my fault. I tried to hide from God. I thought He was ashamed of me because of the events the week before David's death. I tried to target something specific in my mind that I did to make David kill himself. Then I could ask forgiveness and be released from my guilt and condemnation.

I thought, *God knows this is my fault and He's going to bring it out in the open somehow. Then I'm really in trouble.*

I believe my shame and guilt after David's suicide kept me from God's presence for a longer time. I don't really understand how the whole process of my relationship with God was restored. All I can say is, it was a work accomplished by the Holy Spirit and my choice to allow Him to heal me. I struggled not only with the sense of shame and abandonment by God in a place of darkness, but the loss of my devotional life in daily Bible reading, prayer, and talking with God.

The darkness I felt intensified because my spirit was not being nurtured. The force of the blow from David's suicide and the tremendous amount of energy it took for me to work through my grief daily left me with little energy to do anything else. Not only did I not have the energy, but I had no desire to pray or read. I knew I needed to do these things, but I couldn't. I desperately wanted God to be there.

> I was thinking this morning about my relationship with God, and I feel like it's gone. I feel so far away. I try to read my Bible, and it just doesn't seem to have relevance for me, although I know it should. The words are empty. Do I still have faith?
>
> Journal Entry,
> September 18, 1997

As the anger and pain diminished, I began to take small steps of renewed faith. I picked up my Bible, thumbed through it, and put it back down. For me to pick it up and hold it was a huge step. I took what for some may seem like insignificant steps, but for me they were giant strides. I had to give myself credit for even picking up my Bible. Coming through such a difficult time of pain, anger, and disillusionment not only with my husband but also with God — it was a big step of faith to turn to God when things still did not make sense.

God honored every step of faith I took and met me where I was. I believe it was when I took those small steps that God met me. It was in the meeting place that He deposited within me the desire and the ability to meet with Him again.

I desperately wanted the ability to listen to God, to hear His voice speaking again, but I had a decision to make. When my emotions calmed, I developed more awareness that I was at a crossroads of decision. Would I choose to continue my walk with God and allow Him deeper into my situation, even though nothing in life made sense? Or would I reject Him and walk a road of bitterness toward Him?

> Deep in my heart I've been feeling like I'm at a crossroads of decision. It's as if my heart has been weighing whether I really believed in God and if I was going to walk on with Him. I want to be close to God. I want to have a deep abiding relationship with Him. Although during this time in my life I've felt so reckless and out of control, I know that God's mercy and grace have covered me and kept me. I'll never understand just how great God's love and mercy are toward me. My heart has said, "Yes, I'll walk on with God."
>
> Journal Entry,
> May 30, 1997

When I made that decision, *Yes, I'm going to walk on with God,* I became keenly aware of how much I wanted God, how desperately I needed Him.

In my desperation I tried to attend more services at church. I knew I needed to be in God's presence whether or not I felt Him. I knew it was in the presence of God that healing would take place.

I had a difficult time going to church in the beginning; I felt out of place.

I felt as if people were watching me and blaming me as well. When I did go, I found a new place to sit. It was on the opposite side from where David and I usually sat. I sat in the front row. I did not want to see anyone looking at me.

No one came and sat with me, partly because people don't like to sit on the front row at church. I found out later, when people shared with me, that they felt as if they wanted to come sit with me but did not know what to say or do.

I told them, "It's okay to come and sit with me. You don't have to say or do anything."

I told them I knew they were there because of their desire to show love and support; yet in spite of such support, I felt out of place in church for more than a year.

I fidget when I go to church, often finding it difficult to stay in my seat for a two-hour service. I have even had to get up and walk out at times, often feeling, *What's the use in going to church?* When I listen to God's word through a message or reading my Bible, it just doesn't have the same effect on me as it once did. It doesn't grab hold of me the way it used to. I still feel lost in church, unable to quite find my place.

Journal Entry,
April 4, 1997

In the beginning I did not participate in any church activities, and it was rare that I participated in prayer times. One Sunday in a church service we had prayer groups, and I took a step to make myself participate.

A lady in my prayer group said to me, "God is saying that He wants you to come to church more. He wants you to read your Bible more and pray more."

Right after she said that, I dropped hands with the people around me and said, "I disagree — and if you weren't so busy listening to God for my life, maybe you could hear Him for your own life!"

I walked away from the prayer circle. I was so angry at the time, I had to walk away before something more came out of my mouth.

God knew where I was in life. He was in control, although I did not sense it. He knew I had little ability to pray, read, or go to church. A word from God in times of grief should never provoke anger or condemnation. It should always promote grace, healing, and comfort.

Not being able to sense God's presence is the darkest time I have ever experienced in my life. Although I was not aware of it during my grief, the only thing that was not gone from my life and that sustained me was

Christ within me. Looking back now, I can say it, but going through it, everything within my mind, will, and emotions said God was gone.

I began my walk with what I call a "Foot of the Cross Experience." The Gospels record the crucifixion of Christ and the events that unfolded in this manner:

> *And when the sixth hour had come (about midday), there was darkness over the whole land until the ninth hour. And at the ninth hour Jesus cried with a loud voice, "Eloi, Eloi, lama sabachthani?" which means, My God, My God, why have you forsaken me — deserting me and leaving me helpless and abandoned?* (Mk. 15:33-34, Amplified)
>
> *Some women were watching from a distance. Among them were Mary Magdalene, Mary the mother of James the younger...In Galilee these women had followed him and cared for his needs. Many other women who had come up with him to Jerusalem were also there.* (Mk. 15:40 NIV)

Here was Jesus, the One in Whom these men and women had placed all of their hopes and dreams about the Kingdom of God being fulfilled here on earth. Here He was hanging on a cross with darkness surrounding them. They must have been disillusioned, disoriented, and surely questioned, *Why?* All they were living for was dying — being crucified before their very eyes.

The men and women who were there watching Jesus were forced to walk through the events that unfolded. They removed the body of Jesus and buried Him. They must have searched deeply and intently about what they were going to do next. They must have grieved intensely over the loss of their entire livelihood.

It was much the same way for me after my husband's suicide. All my dreams and what I was living for were gone — dead before my eyes. All I could do was be in the darkness and watch as the painful events unfolded before me. I was required to embrace all the doubts, questions, and fears I had and take a risk — walk forward, hoping that God was really there...somewhere.

The good news about a "Foot of the Cross Experience" was that resurrection day came, and the people were given new hope. My resurrection day came as well. As my healing came, I was again able to sense the presence of God when I made a choice to allow Him deeper into my darkness.

I have come to realize it was because of the magnitude of my emotional state that I was unable to sense God's presence for a time. I was in a protective emotional state, and I shut out everything around me. It is how God created us to deal with traumatic grief and loss. I slowly developed an internal awareness that God loved me unconditionally. God did not blame me, but He knew the place of pain I was in, and He wanted to heal me. I started to develop my devotional life again, and I returned to church on a regular basis.

Attending church was only part of the first step. When I went to church and listened to sermons, I wrestled with thoughts, *What is faith? What is life? What is my life for?*

Deep down I knew God really existed, but I was forced to confront the question. I knew God was there somewhere, or I would not be searching so desperately for Him. It was my relationship and my foundation with God before David's suicide that continually nudged me and reminded me that He was there. It was encouragement from Corrie, my friends, and my pastors that God was still with me and had a plan for my life.

In my search to find God I went to church hoping to hear something that allowed me to find Him. I read my Bible. I read books in hope of finding God somewhere. I searched intensely in all my external resources. Then one day in a counseling session Corrie said something to me about communing with God, and a light went on within me.

Christ dwells within my heart! The Spirit of the living God abides in me.

I realized my emotions were no longer these tempestuous storms raging within me, and I had the ability to quiet my soul and listen to God.

As I practiced listening more, I sensed more and more of God's presence surrounding me. I heard the voice of God gently speaking to my heart again. It opened up a new venue for talking with God. I was able to hear Him with more clarity than ever before. For the first time in a year, I felt His presence around me, and I heard Him speak to me.

> I heard the gentle whisper of His Spirit softly say, "It's time to come back. It's time to draw near." I felt His presence all weekend long! Hearing and sensing His soft whisper calling to the depths of my soul, it is so

refreshing! Like the refreshing smell of a
moist spring morning when you just want to
keep breathing in the smell of earthen pine
— taking in as much as you can hold. The
depth of the Spirit of God calling to the depth
of my spirit — drawing me, calling me again.
Deep calling unto deep.

Journal Entry,
July 24, 1997

My spirit responded to the call of God. Now I
wanted God even more. Now I knew God was there,
and I began to trust Him even though everything in my
life said, *What for?*

I discovered that is what faith is — trusting that God
is in control when every arena of my life feels out of control. Corrie shared with me that she saw more of the Spirit
of Christ, more faith in my life during my struggles with
redefining my faith than she heard on the tape of David's
funeral when I spoke.

The character of Who God is and His love for me
became evident as I walked out my life. My own character
was transformed. I became a living epistle — with the hand-
writing of God's grace and healing upon my life. It was
evident to everyone around me.

As I kept going to church and allowed myself to sit in
the presence of God, I noticed I would leave church with
a little more peace in my soul than I had when I came. It
was in the presence of God that the greatest work of inner
healing took place and a renewed sense of belonging came.

I went to church this morning, and thank You, Lord, for the first time since David's death I felt a sense of belonging to my church! The church family, I felt loved today, I felt the presence of God greatly today! I wonder what it is that God is doing in my heart. What direction is He pointing me toward in life? I think that in some way God is going to begin to use this dark season in my life to bring healing and hope to many around me.

Journal Entry,
December 21, 1997

Although it was not without the pain and grief of the adjustments in my life, the wind of God's Spirit continued to gently blow away the ashes of my grief. I continued to sense God's presence, and I had glimpses of new hope, faith, and confidence in life.

As I searched for God, although I am still searching to find Him and to know Him more, I came to a place where I questioned if the call of God was still present within my life. I came to a place where I wondered what my life was all about and what I was to do with it.

What am I supposed to do with this thing called life? This has been a pivotal turning point after my husband's suicide. A good friend of mine and leader within my church prayed over me and said that God's calling has not left me and I was still called to teach. It gave me a glimmer of hope. It confirmed what my pastor told me after my aunt's funeral, that no matter what one goes through in life

    — tragic circumstances, the grief and sorrow life can throw your way

    — the call of God persists no matter what.

Journal Entry,
March 5, 1997

My perspective on life and God was being redefined. I realized God is much bigger than I ever imagined. I wanted my life to have meaning, and only knowing God more intimately could fulfill that desire.

A season of searching to know God more gripped my heart. I struggled with finding God, trying to communicate with Him. I cried out to Him much of the time in tears. When my words failed, the tears came. What I perceived as the silence of God, coupled with a new desire to know Him and the desperately dark and lonely times, provoked a deeper search for Him.

The inner transformation that had taken place over the last few years was manifesting outwardly. My whole demeanor changed, and I sensed people were more comfortable talking with me. I opened myself up to others and took more initiative to talk with them.

I found I was standing more confidently in life, with the assurance that the Lord was by my side. I found God and recognized that He was always with me, that

He never left me nor did He forsake me. He kept me, carried me, and brought me into a new life with Him.

New dreams and desires came alive in my heart. I realized that the opportunities and possibilities in life are endless. Healing came to my heart but not without a price. It left scars, but it is the scars of life circumstances that give me the greatest understanding, compassion, and ability to minister to others. I believe making it through such a difficult season in life is not evidence of how strong I am, but how strong and faithful God is.

My pastors and Corrie helped to facilitate my reintegration to life by identifying situations I could become involved in. There were small tasks I took on in church, in work, and in my social life, but they were big steps in beginning to live again. I thank God there were people I trusted who spoke words of wisdom and encouragement, allowing me to break through to another dimension of my new life.

From the darkness of the valley, the sun began to rise, and light began to shine again. God deposited a large amount of grace in my life. He gave me a new confidence that no matter what circumstances come my way, He is always there. He created in me a new desire to minister grace, healing, and compassion to people who are hurting. I will never be the same.

> The Lord spoke this to me in my quiet time with Him, "When you return, strengthen your brothers." When Jesus spoke this to the Apostle Peter, He knew the struggles that Peter would go through after

he denied the Lord. Jesus knew that Peter would go through a lot, then return in an even stronger grace and understanding of who God is, and an even more intimate relationship with Jesus.

When I return, I hope the Lord will use me to strengthen those around me. I pray this season in my life will not be in vain.

Journal Entry,
November 14, 1997

Chapter Seven

Grieving Rituals And New Traditions

There is a time for everything,
and a season for every activity under heaven.
— Ecclesiastes 3: 1

Yesterday was the first anniversary of David's death. I can't believe it's been one year since he's been gone. I went to the cemetery and stayed for about two hours.

I sat in front of his grave and just talked to David. I told him how much he hurt me by taking his own life. I told him what an almost impossible road I have had to walk this past year because of him. I told him how angry I was at him several times, but that I still loved him and missed him very much. I told him all the hopes and dreams we had together were now buried with him.

I said, "Good-bye, David. I love you."
Journal Entry,
August 13, 1997

Early on in my grief I established grieving rituals important in my healing process. Every birthday, holiday, and anniversary date of his death, I brought flowers to the cemetery and talked to David.

Several disagreed with my rituals and asked, "Why do you go to the cemetery? He's not there. He's with the Lord. Just rejoice that he is in a better place."

It made me feel guilty at first, but Corrie helped me see that these rituals brought a sense of closure. I needed them. When I went to the cemetery, I felt as if David could hear every word I said. I cleaned the headstone and watered the plants. I always brought him one red rose, because he had always bought me roses. One red rose always symbolized our love for each other.

On the second anniversary of David's death I thought about not going to the cemetery, but I could not stay away. I just did not want to go alone. I called Corrie on Monday two days before the anniversary of David's suicide, and told her I needed to go to the cemetery but did not want to go alone.

She said, "Let me see what I can do to change my schedule around and I'll meet you there."

A miracle happened. She changed her schedule, and met me at the cemetery. What a moment of truth it was. For the first time I saw David's name engraved on the headstone with the dates of his birth and death.

Although I had been living without him the past two years, there it read in black and white, no denying it: *David J. Rodrigues, Born December 6th, 1952, Died August 12th, 1996.*

It was true. My husband's body lay in the ground.

Corrie and I sat down in front of his grave and talked about his suicide. We looked at the headstone of this person we talked about for two years. I cried and looked into Corrie's eyes.

Her facial expression said it all. *Yes, it's really true. He's gone. This is his grave.*

The time I spent with Corrie sitting in front of David's grave brought more inner healing. I felt something release me. I felt safe with her there. I finally felt at peace inside, and it gave me the courage to go back on the anniversary date — alone.

I arrived and sat down in front of his grave. I just stared at his name and began talking to him. I told him I was finally able to forgive him and to forgive myself. I stayed for a few hours. I didn't cry. I just sat there and talked to him periodically. When I did finally leave, I felt released and freedom within my soul to move on with my life.

It didn't take away the moments that I still think about him, and I cry because I miss him, but when those moments come, they come with a great love that wells up within me and says, "David, I loved you. I

will always love you. You will always hold a
very special place within my heart.

Journal Entry,
August 12, 1998

My rituals of going to the cemetery did help me
gain a sense of closure with David's death. On his birth-
days and our wedding anniversary I bought cards and
wrote letters to him inside. On those dates I took fresh
flowers to his grave.

As healing came, the inclination to go to the cemetery lessened. By the third wedding anniversary I did
not go and felt okay about it.

The anniversaries of special dates and of his death
always bring changes to my emotions. It has been less
emotional over time for most of the special dates except
the anniversary of his death, which stirs much emotion
in me. It is as if I'm back in a grieving mode for a time.
Most people no longer remember that it is the anniversary of his death, but it is etched with fire in my heart
and mind. I know that date will bring memories for a
long time to come, but I have no doubt that as the years
go on, I will move through that time a bit more easily.

Another grieving ritual for two years was attending
a Catholic mass with a friend of mine and having David
mentioned in the prayers. It was a ritual I was not accustomed to nor that I continued, but at the time it brought
me peace.

The yearly holiday traditions David and I had came
as a challenge for me. We always spent one holiday with

my family and one with his family. When the holidays came, I felt lost and did not know what to do.

Corrie and I talked about establishing new traditions that were uniquely mine. When the first set of holidays came, the grieving remained quite intense, so I spent Thanksgiving with my mother and Christmas with my father. This time proved lonely and difficult for me, but I had to start somewhere.

Here it is Christmas evening. All the kids and my brothers are gone now. My dad and his wife have gone to bed, and here I am. I'm sitting here alone and thinking about the past several months, the tremendous amount of pain and turmoil that has accompanied them.

As the world around me goes on with joy during these holidays, I wonder if I will have joy again during my favorite time of year. It felt rather bizarre today as I sat alone with no one at my side. I just observed everyone moving through the motions of the holiday season. I was in the middle of a lot of people, my family, but felt like an observer. Now that it's over, I think the holidays are no big deal. Will things get easier as time goes on? How long does it take to become accustomed to being alone during these times?

Journal Entry,
December 25, 1996

During the second and third holiday seasons I made changes. I participated in a Christmas ritual at Hospice of the Valley by bringing a special ornament to hang on the Christmas tree in memory of David. I felt good about being able to honor my husband, to say to him in some way, *You were important to me, and I want others to know about you.* I did something good born out of tragedy.

I bought new decorations and a Christmas tree. I put up Christmas lights and tried to regain some of the joy the holidays had always brought. I tried to remember, especially around Christmas time, the spiritual meaning of the celebration — the birth of my Savior.

I enjoyed being with my family and developed a new thankfulness for being able to share the joy of the holidays with them. Since the first year of holidays passed, I have regained my excitement and joy about that time of year. I try not to look at the holidays as a time of loneliness but as a time to love and give to others, a time to be loved by others.

During these times I still have days when I feel lonely. It is almost inevitable for any single person or anyone who has lost a loved one. When I sense myself becoming depressed, I try to find things that bring me joy and concentrate on them.

Another tradition I established for myself is getting up every morning, no matter how I feel, and thanking God for my family, my church family, my home, and being alive. I still have bad days no matter how grateful I say I am, but it is just part of being human. I know the day will pass, and a new day is coming.

I buy fresh flowers and keep them in a vase in my living room where I can see them every morning and evening. I watch the buds blossom over time. The beauty of the flowers reminds me that God watches my life as it blossoms before Him. The blossoming flowers remind me daily that changes in life take time.

I continue to journal my thoughts, and when I read through some of my journals, it is a testimony to myself of God's faithfulness. I am amazed by how far He has brought me, and it always brings praises to my lips.

My cat Sierra and I have a special tradition every morning. I get my cup of coffee and sit in my chair with a pillow on my lap. Sierra climbs on the pillow, curls up in a ball, puts her head near my chest, and sleeps a little while longer.

I get together with "the girls" once a month for a night out of fat food, laughs, and giggles. I have found it is the little things in life that often bring me the greatest peace and joy. I try giving people more hugs and telling my family and others that I love them. Given the uncertainty of life, with every opportunity I tell people they are loved and special.

I now collect lighthouses. Some are pictures, and others are ceramic pieces. It reminds me that during the midst of my life's most intense storm, God saved me, and He sent Corrie as a beacon of light. She carried my faith for a season, helping me find my way back to God and back to my path in life.

I try to meditate on God's Word and think on good things especially during times of the year that I know are most difficult for me. I try to daily spend quiet time before God, read my Bible, pray, and just listen to God. It keeps me spiritually in tune when my emotions try to create an imbalance.

Although for some the grieving rituals and traditions I established seem strange and silly, they have brought healing and given new meaning to my life. I have realized that my life is fun if I make it that way. My life has meaning depending upon my attitude and willingness to embrace what I already have and the new things that God brings me. I am trying to lighten up and enjoy life again. I have experienced enough darkness and sadness to last two lifetimes. I have joy and laughter, and the light of God now shines.

The prophet Isaiah said it perfectly: "Arise, shine for your light has come, and the glory of the Lord rises upon you." (Isaiah 60:1)

Chapter Eight

Memories And Good-Byes

The time has come for me to
release you into God's hands.
The Lord has kept me,
And now I'm able to stand.
Although you're gone in body,
The love I hold for you
Can never be taken away;
Your memory will live on
In my heart,
And never be far away.

— C.M. Rodrigues

"Memories — tender, loving, bittersweet. They can never be taken from you. Nothing can detract from the joy and the beauty you and your loved one shared. The memories are yours to keep."[1]

My memories of my life with David are truly bittersweet. They have required me to grieve for the loss of a life cut short and the loss of a life once anticipated.

The passage of time has been long enough now that I no longer have the haunting memories of finding him, although the memory is available at any fleeting moment.

I have more good thoughts and memories than I do bad, and many things in my daily life trigger memories of David. The smell of a certain cologne, and I am instantly transported back to active conversations with David about it. I pass by certain restaurants and remember what he always ordered. When I eat certain foods, it reminds me of how much he loved to eat sweets, most of all eggnog during the Christmas season. Seeing certain types of clothing others wear, I think about the times we went shopping.

Seeing someone in an electric wheelchair in the mall, I immediately think about the fun times we had in the malls. David loved to go racing through them. I also think of the difficulty that the person in the wheelchair has in his or her daily life. It brings memories of the daily struggles with attendant care, wheelchair troubles, bladder infections, and van electric lift troubles. My compassion goes out to them. I know all too well their daily life challenges.

I go to church and see the place where David liked to sit on the end aisle. It is empty, but the memories of watching him worship God with his eyes closed, almost as if he were dancing with God, warm my heart because now he is dancing with God.

When I see others in church who are disabled in any way, it brings memories of the hope David always held onto of being healed, the anticipation he held every time he went to a service: "Maybe today is the day I will get up from this wheelchair."

It brings back the memories of crushed anticipation when we went home and he was still in his wheelchair, unable to move. It brings back the conversations we had when we declared in our hearts that whether David was healed or not, God was still sovereign and still the ultimate Healer. We resolved to love God and trust Him even if it did not make sense.

The memories of the dreams we held in our hearts for our life together all seem but a distant shadow now. I have come to a place of realization that I have to let go of the memories with both hands, no clinging, even with a little finger. It is my memories and dreams that have the greatest potential for holding me back both now and in the future if I don't let go. It is not an easy thing to do; it is a scary thing to do. I am letting go of the familiar and simply reaching out to the future with no idea of what's ahead.

It requires me to reverberate what the prophet Isaiah said: "Forget the former things; do not dwell on the past. See, I am doing a new thing! Now it springs up; do you not perceive it? I am making a way in the desert and streams in the wasteland." (Isaiah 43: 18-19)

It was my memories of what God did for me in the past that kept me going through the darkness. Now it is my new encounters with God that give me the greatest hope and anticipation for my future. My memories of my relationship with God, how I related to Him, how I talked to Him, how He worked through my life, have all changed. I am constantly reminded that all of who I was, is now changed forever — even my relationship with God.

It was Corrie who continually reminded me that my old ways of communing with God were just that — old. She reminded me that God was teaching me new ways to find Him, new ways to hear Him, new ways to walk with Him.

Letting go of old memories forces me to confront and reflect within myself what it is that I want my life to be in the future. What are the new dreams that I can begin to have and hold out before God as I walk on in life with Him? I must begin to have a vision of my own destiny in life and create my own memories of my life now. I must anticipate God's goodness for me in my future. It is all a step of faith.

I stand before God facing life, my hands untied, outstretched to heaven, saying, "God, give me a new vision in life. Show me how to dream new dreams and create new memories in my life. Help me to walk down the path that is my destiny."

With each new day that dawns and each time I embrace a new dream, I say good-bye to David just a little bit more. Saying good-bye after a spouse's suicide is not something that happens overnight. It is a gradual process. It is a painful process but one of freedom as well. As the past Seven years following David's death have come to a close, I have realized I can never say good-bye with words. In my heart and in my own way I have said and continue to say good-bye to David.

I first had to accept that I could not have done or said anything that would have prevented his suicide. Then

I had to let David go from the grip I held him in, in my heart, and place him into God's hands. It was one of the most difficult and painful steps of faith and trust I have ever taken, but it was a necessary one if I wanted to move on in life.

Saying good-bye to David and my life I had with him does not mean that I am erasing him from my heart memories. It just means that I am ready to move on with my own life. I am truly grateful for the years I had with him. Those years helped to shape me and form my character, all a part of who I am today. It is the memories and the lessons of yesterday that God is using to shape and plan my tomorrows.

When I am with others who knew David, I often hear their own memories of him as they recall times when he brought encouragement to them. I sense the loss they feel in their own hearts but also the grateful-ness for their relationship with David. When I hear others talk about him and what he brought to their lives, it inevitably makes me reflect upon my own life and how I live it.

Ultimately, when I die, the only things that will be left behind are my relationships with others and how my life affected them. I think about how I treat others and what I want my life to be remembered for. Sharing my memories of David with Corrie and other close friends and family has helped to bring healing to all whose lives David touched.

When I think about "the act" of saying good-bye to someone, we both stand facing each other waving and saying good-bye. It is not until one actually turns and begins walking away that one gets anywhere.

Similarly, I have stood stationary with tears streaming down my face, waving and saying good-bye, long enough. I have turned. God has wiped the tears from my eyes, my vision is clearing, and I am beginning to walk down my own path in life. Turning brought pain; taking the first step brought agony. Now, with every little step I take, it becomes less painful and more hopeful for the future.

The word *good-bye* seems to have a ring of finality to it, so I will just say, "David, I'll see you soon."

When the time comes for the Lord to call me home, I know without a shadow of a doubt I will see David walking with the Lord. His memory and my love for him will live on in my heart forever. In saying good-bye to David, I have said hello to my new life, whatever it may hold.

As Henry David Thoreau said, "The future is worth expecting."

Chapter Nine

A Season Of Singleness

Do not be afraid; you will not suffer shame.
Do not fear disgrace; you will not be humiliated.
You will forget the shame of your youth and
Remember no more the reproach of your widowhood.
For your Maker is your husband —
The Lord Almighty is his name —
The Holy One of Israel is your Redeemer,
He is called the God of all the Earth.
— Isaiah 54: 4-5

Where do I go from here? I guess I'm at
a point where I have to decide that I'm really going to go on with my life, that I'm
really going to try to find my life again. I
have come to a point where I'm aware that
my personal intimate life is different. Where
once I was in union and free to be a lover to
the man God had given me as my husband,
now I'm alone.

What do I do when I feel the need to be held? Where do I place all those intimate emotions that I was once able to freely express with my husband? Now all of a sudden there is no one to direct them toward! Where do I place them? What do I do with them? I can only imagine that at times they will become stronger as reality continues to settle in upon me of what it is that's missing.

I've become more aware of the dreams and visions that have died and been buried right along with David. I've become more aware that after ten years of my life being shared with someone — I'm single again.

Journal Entry
August 9, 1997

A gaping hole now exists in my life, and all my needs once met by my husband I now perceive as a longing unfulfilled. My companion, my lover, my best friend, and my center of life other than Jesus is gone. I'm walking on the path of life, single again.

The first time someone mentioned being single was the day of the funeral — of all days.

She said, "Oh, don't worry. You're young and pretty. You'll find someone else."

I wanted to hit her. I was not worried about it or thinking about it at the time.

Frequently within the first two years of grieving, when people said anything to me about being young and finding someone else, it provoked anger. I was still angry at David and grieving my loss. I did not want to think about having another man in my life who could do the same thing to me. People still mention it, but I don't pay too much attention. It doesn't provoke anger as it did before; healing and forgiveness made that possible.

My transition into singleness can be described by one word — awareness. My awareness of singleness and the unique things I faced came over time.

Initially I faced what now seem like trivial things: *What do I do with my wedding ring? Do I keep wearing it, put it on my right finger, or take it off completely? What do I do with David's rings? What do I do with David's clothes and all his favorite things? Where am I going to live?*

In the middle of intense grieving these things seem like huge mountains of decision at the moment.

I felt so angry at David that I took my wedding ring off for a few days, but the anguish and pain were too deep. I could not leave it off. I needed to put it back on. It was all I had left. Eventually I decided to keep wearing my wedding ring on my left hand, and after about a year I switched to the right finger. Then I replaced it with another ring on my right hand. After two years I put it away in a jewelry box.

I kept all David's rings and jewelry. I have them put away also. I am still unsure of what to do with all of it. I kept some of his favorite sweaters, and I wear them sometimes. They seem to still have his smell on them.

Going through David's clothes was an agonizing process. With every piece of clothing that went into a box or a bag, I was slapped in the face by the reality that my husband was gone and not coming back. I kept his jewelry box and some of his favorite things, all packed away in boxes. I imagine one day I will part with them.

Occasionally, those things still make me cry.

Sometimes I think, *These are things that no one can take away from me and I'm not going to give them up.*

As a suicide survivor so many things were just ripped from me that I think this is one thing I can have a little control over in my life. It is still an area of healing that needs to take place.

Three months after David's death I moved out of our house to a one-bedroom condo. I needed to move out quickly. It tortured me every time I came home. When I walked into the house, the events of the evening I found him replayed in my mind. Every time I walked into our bedroom, I burst into tears. His smell lingered in the room, but he was gone. The house remained empty, just me and my dog. After I moved, I still came home to emptiness and decisions about what to do with my time, but the agonizing images lessened.

When I began living alone, I became aware that I now had to make all my life decisions alone. I still wrestle with whether I make the right decisions. I realized that I relied a lot on David to make major decisions in our lives. During the first year after his death, my judgment and reasoning were poor, and I needed a lot of help in those areas.

I talked a lot with Corrie and my pastors about major issues that surfaced, such as moving in with a room-mate, buying a house with someone, and moving to a different geographical location. They helped me by listening and asking me the right questions to guide me. I needed people of sound wisdom and a perspective larger than mine to see things clearly and make wise choices.

I remember the one time I did not ask someone to help me about making the decision to buy a new car.

I thought, *I can do this myself. I don't need someone for every little thing in my life.*

I was wrong. What a mistake!

I went into a car dealership and talked with a salesman about buying a new sports car. He became quite excited about his prospective commission on the sale. We went back and forth about the price. Then I told him I would think about it and let him know.

He said, "I'll call another dealer and get the car here for you. Just leave me a check for twenty-five thousand dollars."

I did! I didn't even have two hundred dollars in my checking account.

Then I went home, thought about it, and changed my mind. I did not want that car.

I went back to get my check and realized he had the car there at the lot. When I told him I did not want the car, he flew into a rage and refused to give me my check.

I went to my mom and explained to her what had happened, the bad decision I made, and she went with me to the dealership. She tried to explain to the salesman that I really was not in my right mind, because I had just lost my husband, but he did not want to hear it. He flew into another rage and yelled at both of us. He threw his arms up in the air, his face turned red with anger, and he paced behind his desk.

My mom said, "Look, if you don't give me the check, I'll call the police, and we'll get it that way."

The manager of the car lot came over, and we eventually got back my check — not that it was good for the money. It wasn't.

"Carolyn," my mom asked, "why didn't you tell me you were coming here? I would have come with you, or we could have called someone to help you."

I eventually did buy a new car. I got a good deal on a beautiful burgundy sports car with a sun roof and gold wheels.

I've learned to pray and wait on my decisions until I have peace about them. Frequently I ask for insight from my pastor, his wife, or others I know I can trust. I have also learned how to sense the leading of the Holy Spirit in making decisions. God has taught me and is still teaching me when I pray, how to wait upon Him, listen, and allow Him to direct me in the right way.

I eventually became aware that I had responsibility for my own life. I have responsibility for how I take care of myself physically, spiritually, emotionally, and socially. Initially I was so depressed that I really did not care about any of these things.

As I worked through my grief and walked it out, I walked myself right into a place of isolation. I felt myself withdraw from people and the world around me. Living alone, the easiest thing to do was withdraw. I was scared, lonely, and had no confidence in life, God, or myself.

Sometimes I want to just step out and be free, be able to fly again in life! Other times I just peek out, and the world seems like a big scary place, and I just retreat back in right away. I go to the farthest corner of this cocoon that I live in and just sit down and wait. For what? I don't know. What am I waiting for? What's keeping me in here?

Journal Entry
June 8, 1998

Almost two years after David's suicide, within one month of each other, Corrie and my pastor both spoke something into my life. Their words helped to draw me out of the place of isolation and propel me into a new place.

In a counseling session Corrie said to me, "It's time to take responsibility for your own life. You are responsible for living your own life now. David is no longer a responsibility that you carry."

I knew she was right. It was time to take responsibility for my life and move on.

During a Sunday-morning church service my pastor shocked me and said, "Carolyn, life would like to shut you out and keep you back in a dark cave. God has good things for you ahead."

When he said that, something within me resounded, *That's right! I'm not going to stay in this dark cave, hidden any longer.*

Both of those words spoken were full of wisdom and, most important, accurate timing. I was in a place in life where I could receive what they said. I made a choice at those moments to move on and not let anything keep me back.

I still have my whole life ahead of me, and I won't be cheated out of my life.

It was a major turning point for me, and I allowed myself, sometimes made myself, become more involved in social activities, church activities, and family gatherings.

As I went out with others more frequently and spent time with them, I gained more of a sense that I was still part of this life. I became more open and sociable in my conversation with others, because I did not have David to rely on to talk to others.

As I continued to open myself up to others, my confidence in life grew. Now I can open a conversation with anyone and feel completely comfortable talking with them. I've discovered that whether others are single or married, people are looking to have friendships — trusting relationships with others who will accept them for who they are and not judge them.

I have also discovered the importance of choosing my closest friends wisely. To them I am accountable and can share my struggles and successes, knowing that they will bring correction if needed; support, encouragement, and prayer all the time. It is a close friendship that develops into a deep abiding relationship — a kindred-spirit relationship. This is a rare find in life but something to be treasured.

Another major issue of singleness that I confronted after David's suicide is "dating," along with the thought of ever being married again.

Initially I thought, *I'm never getting married again. I don't want to go through this ever again. I don't think I can trust anyone ever again. I won't give anyone the chance to hurt me like this ever again.*

These thoughts were born out of my grief, anger, and pain.

However, in the later months of my recovery Corrie said to me, "I want you to think about something. Think about it being better to have loved and lost than to never have had the opportunity to love."

That made me think about all the good things that came from my marriage to David. The things that he deposited into my life can never be taken away. He taught me a lot about faith, love, courage, tenacity, and strength. I learned to love and look beyond physical, tangible circumstances — into the deep hidden character of the soul God created. I am grateful for the time God gave me with David.

All the good times and good things that remain in my heart have helped me to decide, *Yes, I'm willing to love again the one whom God chooses to send.*

I have to remind myself that although more than 30,000 people commit suicide each year, and although I went through a second suicide within my family a year after David's, it is relatively rare that it will happen again in my lifetime. If it does, God will enable me to walk through it again. I don't say this with an arrogant attitude but one of "knowing from experience" that God is faithful. He will carry me through any kind of circumstance that life brings my way. I allowed God to bring healing into my life, and it continues to this day.

I will probably experience apprehension when I do become involved in a relationship — wondering if I will be judged about the suicide or if he will run away. If that happens, then I know he is not the one whom God has chosen.

I am not in any hurry to marry again, but I'm not closed to it either. I have chosen to view this time of singleness as a rare opportunity of which to take full advantage. I have the opportunity to spend time with God and develop my personal intimate life with Jesus as never before. As a woman being married, then single again, I have realized that the deepest yearnings in my soul and spirit can be met only partially by a man.

The longing to be cherished, honored, and loved for who I am without any pretense; the longing to be taken care of and not worrying about my life — there is a place within me that can be filled only by God. That place of fulfillment is being in union with Christ. There is also a part of me that longs to have a companion in my life. When the three are joined together, it brings a richer sense of being fulfilled in life, with the ultimate fulfillment to come when we are all joined together with Christ in heaven.

I believe God created each of us with an empty place that can be satisfied only by Him. Otherwise, we would probably not seek to know Him and the fulfillment that only He can bring to us.

I have the opportunity to become focused in life, set goals, dream new dreams, and pursue them with all my heart. It does not mean that I don't get lonely, but when I do, I focus on the Lord and praise Him for my life now. I thank Him that I am still alive and that I have my whole life in front of me. I try to turn my attention to others in need and fill the loneliness with servitude. I look to others in need and trust that God will touch them through me. It takes away some of the loneliness and self-pity.

For the areas of deep emotional needs I often cry out to God in my prayer time. I tell Him what I am feeling. I spend time with Him and allow Him to minister to me. I focus my attention on His goodness and praise Him for what He has done in my life. I come away with the sense that He knows the depth of my needs and everything is going to be all right.

I come away with peace and solitude within my soul, able to say with assurance, *God is faithful, and He is in control of my life.*

I still struggle with loneliness and thoughts that I am going to be alone for the rest of my life or that no one will ever love me again. During those times I run to God, or I share with my closest friends the struggles that I am experiencing, and I get prayer for them. Whether I talk to God or my friends, getting the thoughts out in the open allows me to gain a sense of perspective so that I can move through those difficult times.

I look ahead now during this season of singleness, and can say, *God, I want to become all that You have destined me to be.*

I know with God all things are possible in my life. I can do anything I want. I can fulfill the new dreams that are within my heart. Tragedies and circumstances will always try to keep me down, but with the Lord by my side I can soar again.

In my transition into singleness the Lord has brought and is still bringing balance into my life. I can recognize all the good things I have right now — a wonderful family who love me unconditionally; a wonderful church family and friends who are sources of support, encouragement, and much-needed relationships. Most important, I have a new intimate relationship and close friendship with God. I am trusting that until the day He chooses to set someone in my path, He will meet all my needs.

I am grateful to be back on the path that God has destined for me. I am beginning to live again, and I value the life God has given me. I am finding out what my life is all about.

I am finding out who I am. I have come to understand that God knows me by name. I know He loves me for who He created me to be. I don't have to earn or work for His love; He just loves me.

I have learned that He can take care of me, and I don't have to be afraid to move ahead in life. Learning to lean and rely on God does not take away my responsibilities in life, but it gives me the peace and confidence I need to walk through each day. No matter if it is a day when everything goes wrong or a perfect day, I know the Lord is always with me. For now, He is my companion in life.

My birthday was yesterday. I turned thirty-one years old. I guess with all that's happened the past two years, I need to look at the years ahead as a new beginning for my life. Only God can help me to continue moving through any remaining grief, continue to heal my heart, and help me to keep perspective as to where my life is headed. I've begun to dream new dreams and see my life as a world of opportunity. New beginnings....

Journal Entry
March 14, 1998

Chapter Ten

Resolution And Reflections

I will sing of the Lord's great love forever;
with my mouth I will make your
faithfulness known through all generations.
— Psalm 89:1

"What then can separate us from the love of Christ? Shall trouble or hardship or persecution or famine or nakedness or danger or sword?"

Shall suicide?

"No, in all these things we are more than conquerors through him who loved us. For I am convinced that neither death nor life, neither angels nor demons, neither the present nor the future, nor any powers, neither height nor depth, nor anything else in all creation, will be able to separate us from the love of God that is in Christ Jesus our Lord." (Romans 8:35)

I have come to a place where I know nothing has separated or ever will separate me from God's love — not grief, emotions, or anything else that followed my husband's suicide. I have regained a sense of balance in my life, although the work of God's healing continues.

I still think of and search for what my life is all about.

Frequently I think about my question to God, *What is faith?*

The only thing I can remotely attempt to say is that faith begins by recognizing that God is God. He is in control of our lives, but we still have a free will and can make good and bad decisions. I believe one's definition of faith flows out of his personal relationship with Jesus.

I know God kept me guarded in the shadow of His wings in the shelter of the most High during these last five years. He walked me through a transforming journey from shattered brokenness to a vessel restored by His hand. It was not an easy journey. It was not a quick healing. It was not a journey filled with power encounters, dreams, and visions from God. It was a slow, painful, grace-filled process of grief and restoration.

At the lowest points in my life, at the very depth of despair, God came to me through other people. Through others God provided me with the strength I did not have. When I screamed out to God and told Him I was not going to make it, He spoke gently through Corrie and my pastors and said I *was* going to make it. It took someone outside my family and circle of friends to help me gain and keep perspective in my life. When I yelled at God and asked where He was, He came to me through them as they hugged me, held me, and said they were there for me. It is an awesome and powerful lesson of how God can make Himself known to others through our loving and giving to them in a time of need.

I have resolved and relinquished to God the fact that I will never know *why* my husband committed suicide. I still don't have answers for the many questions that initially consumed me: *Is David in hell? Why didn't God warn me? Why did I have to find him?*

I have come to my own conclusion that David's suicide is an open chasm of unanswered questions for me as a survivor. I have learned in my wrestling matches with God that sometimes the greatest peace comes when I give up the right to know everything. Sometimes it is better not to know why rather than knowing and being tormented by the guilt that can follow. There are just some things in life to which I will never have answers, and I am willing to let them rest, allowing God's peace to reign in my heart.

I ultimately have come to a place where I believe and trust that David is with God. He was born again. He loved Jesus, and God's forgiveness spans past, present, and future. I believe we all walk in the forgiveness of God, and David died in God's forgiveness, mercy, and love.

Dr. Billy Graham addressed the issue of suicide in *The Oklahoman Daily*, September 17, 1993. An individual wrote and asked if his uncle lost his salvation because he committed suicide.

Dr. Graham replied, *"No, if the individual truly knew Christ. God understands the mental confusion people face, and although suicide is not the correct solution, God in His mercy has not abandoned the individual."*

Dr. Graham states that we can take comfort in all Christ's promises that nothing will separate us from His great love. *"Just as we cannot be saved by our own good works, but only by what Christ has done for us, neither can we be lost by our bad works if we have honestly committed our lives to Him."*

What a sense of freedom and relief this brings to suicide survivors.

Throughout my journey I have discovered a little of the greatness of Who Jesus really is — the God of the universe and the God of my life. Although He is infinitely paramount, I have learned that He cares for me and loves me for who He made me to be.

Standing at the threshold of life looking out into a huge world was a scary thing for me. It was the first time I had ever really been alone in life. I was scared that my life would crumble again once I stepped out. It was not until I let go of "being in control" and just fell back into God's arms that I had any peace.

I have stepped out of my cocoon and have begun to participate in life. I have stopped watching my life go by, and I have joined it. I am taking new steps and challenges with a bit of trepidation at times but with newfound confidence in God and in life.

When I began to trust God and thank Him for taking care of me, the anxiety, fear, and worry faded away. Peace, confidence, and rest came flooding in. Now, at the times when I find myself desperately lonely, I lie down on my bed. I ask God to put His arms around me, hold me — and I weep in His arms. I am comforted by His presence.

The enduring seasons of my grief drove me into a deeper search for God. They produced stronger, deeper roots of faith in Christ and the completed work of the cross. Through my own inner death I have come to recognize Christ as my true source of life.

Some of the traits of my grieving process were "time," "support," and "choices." From the first day — through the anger, the pain, the guilt, the depression, and the turmoil — it was only the passage of time and support from others that pulled me through. As my emotions settled and I had more control over them, I became more cognizant of my life and the choices I made. I allowed God deeper into my circumstance to heal me. I chose to go on with my life and perceive my life as something valuable and worth living. All these things helped me to arrive at the dawning of a new day in my life.

God is beginning to touch other people's lives through me, both inside and outside the church. As I hear other people's stories, questions arise, and I ponder in my heart. My questions are not those of condescending words but simply an outflow of walking through the aftermath of my husband's suicide. I hope my questions have changed the way I relate to others and how others relate to suicide survivors.

Can we allow others the freedom to grieve? Can we give them the grace and love to experience their emotions and allow the work of grief to take place?

God was not shocked nor was He offended by my grieving and the intense emotions it held. He created the human psyche to deal with traumatic loss through a natural grieving process.

Can we love suicide survivors without being judgmental and critical, assuming the *whys* when no one really knows why? Can we validate and acknowledge the suicide survivor's loss without preaching or using religious clichés? I believe we must come to the suicide survivor as living epistles of God's Word bringing comfort, love, and hope.

Can we not be so careless and sling God's Word around as if it were a quick fix to the tragedies in life? Indeed, God's Word is where we will find healing, but in the difficult circumstances of life we must bring His Word in everyday language and actions to facilitate grace and healing during times of heartbreaking pain.

Can we allow ourselves to be with a grieving person in silence, maybe with just a hug or a human touch? God is able to take His anointing in the presence of pain, anguish, and grief and pour it over the wounded soul and spirit through the human touch.

Have we been so busy trying to "pull ourselves up by the bootstraps of our faith" that somehow, somewhere along the way we have lost our ability to integrate our whole human life experience with our faith? It is by experiences in life that God walks us through the challenges but also strengthens and deepens our faith in Christ.

Can we begin to see our humanness as a process of life transformation into who God has destined us to be? I believe if we allow ourselves to become vulnerable and real with a grieving person, deeper healing takes place in the survivor, and deeper character changes become evident in our own lives. God is not afraid of grief or surprised by how grief works. Neither should we be afraid to allow a person to grieve as long as is necessary to bring complete restoration.

Can we love the grieving person enough not to let him stay in a place of grief, but help him, pray with him, walk with him all the way through to the other side? We have the Book of Life. We may not always have the answers, but we always have God's love, grace, mercy, and compassion available to us.

In reality, all these questions and answers are very practical and real for me as a suicide survivor.

Again, these are the thoughts that I ponder in my heart and no doubt will act upon in my own life. I do not claim to be a scholar in either theology or suicide, but I hope in these chapters a reader will find the testimony of how God can restore a broken life through the comfort we offer. We need one another in this life, not only in difficult circumstances that we must face but also in rejoicing when we have obtained victory over life's battles — when we can be called victorious survivors.

Chapter Eleven

A New Day

See, I am doing a new thing!
Now it springs up; do you not perceive it?
I am making a way in the desert
And streams in the wasteland.
— Isaiah 43:19

New — that word describes how my life has transformed over the last several years.

Each new day that dawns speaks a testimony of God's grace, love, and divine inner healing. Every arena of my life is new. I have a new relationship with God, I have new relationships with my friends, I have a new job, I have new skills and abilities that have emerged, and I live in a new home in a different city. Everything is new.

My relationship with God is completely transformed. Before my husband's death I was defined by people's expectations of me. Now I am defined by who I am in Christ. I have developed new confidence, and I have learned through the journey that my relationship with Christ is *rock solid* — a term I use because it is a portrayal of the completed work of the cross.

When we come to know Jesus as our Savior, we belong to Him, and nothing we face in this life will separate us from Him.

I often find myself meditating on the goodness of God and sending up little prayers like, *Jesus, I miss You. Will You allow me to sense Your presence?*

I always receive an answer as His presence pours over me and surrounds me. The deep desire and hunger for more of Jesus are being fulfilled. Jesus meets me at my heart level and shows me the freedom, the fullness, and the completeness I have in Him. I am a whole and complete person in Christ.

God has taught me to listen inwardly and enjoy freedom outwardly. When I am busy and become caught up in the affairs of daily life, He gently tells me to slow down and give my spirit and my body the rest they require. I find that when I consistently make time to talk to God and meditate on His goodness, the flow of daily life is smoother, and my spirit is able to soar to new heights. He has taught me to celebrate and enjoy the life I have been given.

I absorb the beauty of His creation around me. I enjoy seeing the different shades of green on the mountainsides. I enjoy gazing at the rainbow of colors in the wild flowers around my home. I enjoy breathing in the smell of the ocean and listening to the waves rolling on the shore. I enjoy standing on the oceanside or a mountaintop with the wind blowing over me and through me. My hair is blowing, my clothes are blowing, and my arms are stretched toward heaven. It is the ultimate feeling of being one with Christ.

God has brought new friends into my life. He has shown me the value of relationships. The only thing we take with us when we leave this earth, and the only thing we leave behind, is our relationships with others. We can have many friends, but we can have only a few intimate, close relationships. God has brought friends my way so that no matter what I am going through, I know I can call them any time and for any reason. I can be myself with them, and I trust them completely. My life is enriched by the new friendships that have come into my life.

My professional career transitioned full circle from the medical field into a professional technical arena and back into the medical field. I am now utilizing the teaching mantle that is upon my life, able to meet and interact with many different kinds of people. I enjoy working. It gives me the opportunity to share my testimony with colleagues and direct them to Jesus during the difficult seasons of life.

I have found meaning and purpose at work by finding my calling in God. I am called to serve humanity. I try to lead by example and enable others through my skills to be successful at their jobs. I have discovered that I have strong administrative and business skills. If I can make a difference in one person's life, then I am successful. My life flows out of who I have become.

This new day that I am walking in has brought me new freedom, joy, and peace. It has brought me new perspectives in life. I am no longer bound within the cages of grief. The doors have been unlocked and opened. I have stepped outside the iron gates of pain, anger, guilt, shame, depression, and sadness, stepped into a whole new world.

I am able to see the beauty around me. I choose to be thankful every day that God has blessed me with life. The life that is mine has a destiny over it. I have a purpose and a calling to fulfill. I can walk only one day at a time and let each day unfold its plan and its purpose. It is God's very presence in me that fills me and gives me my purpose in life — to love and serve humanity.

God has called me to look outside my own backyard, to look beyond the four walls of the church. He has called me to look into His heart, to feel His heartbeat, to gaze upon people with His eyes. He has called me to allow Him to filter out all the "stuff" of life — clothes, cars, houses, money — and to see the desperate need of humanity, to be restored into relationship with their Creator Jesus Christ, to be loved and accepted unconditionally. He has called me to have a word of kindness always, to pray for others and watch the power of God transform lives, and to watch new hope fill and overflow the pit of hopelessness in others' lives.

In this new day God is teaching me not to fashion Him in my box according to my experiences but to allow Him to be God.

I look at the desires and dreams in my heart with confidence that God has placed those dreams within me. I take steps daily, and in planning for tomorrow, in order to fulfill those dreams. I want my life to be full and rewarding, so I take steps to make it that way.

I have learned to view the difficult and tragic circumstances that come my way as part of life. Life is unpredictable. There is not much I can do to change things that happen beyond my control. If something happens, I look at the situation and determine if I can do anything to change it. If I need to grieve...I grieve. If I need to cry...I cry. Still I have learned not to stay in the place of grief but to allow the healing power of God to enter my heart and be changed by the process.

Every situation has good and bad components to it. If I can experience the bad, let it go, then allow the good to teach me and transform me, I am fulfilling my destiny in life. Every time I allow a circumstance to change me in a positive way, I can share and teach that to someone else in need. When I see the results of what I share in other people's lives, I am encouraged to continue on.

When I think about my struggles and what other suicide survivors must walk through as they are challenged with their faith in God and restoring their broken lives, I want to hand over all that God has done in my life — but everyone must walk and learn in his or her own journey of life.

I have compiled some suggestions and given some resources for helping suicide survivors walk through the grieving process. A suicide survivor can call any of the numbers listed, and they will provide support groups and agencies in any geographical area that have crisis counseling services. Some of these organizations will send written material about grief after suicide as well.

In this new day I seek to know God more. I must know Him more, because each new day that dawns, I see how God has given me beauty for ashes, turned my mourning into dancing, and given me gladness instead of despair. My life speaks the very essence of Christ's saving grace. It speaks of the availability of His great love and restoring power to all of mankind.

We need only to call out to Jesus. He will embrace us. He will heal us. He will restore us.

End Notes

Chapter 2

¹ Mel Lawrenz and Daniel Green, *Life after Grief* (Grand Rapids: Baker Books, 1995), 14.

² Lawrenz and Green, *Life after Grief,* 14.

Chapter 5

¹ Earl Grollman, *Living When a Loved One has Died* (Boston: Beacon Press, 1995), 5.

² Earl Grollman, *Living When a Loved One has Died,* 29-31.

³ Earl Grollman, *Living When a Loved One has Died,* 47.

Chapter 8

¹ Earl A. Grollman, *Living When a Loved One has Died* (Boston: Beacon Press, 1995), 85.

Appendix

¹ Gary R. Collins, Ph.D., *Christian Counseling* (Dallas: Word publishing, 1988), 354

Appendix

Helps And Suggestions

First Step:
Establish a support team within the church. Have leaders, preferably someone who has a relationship with the survivor, stay in close contact.

Pastors and Leadership:
Help survivors plan and make arrangements for the funeral and/or memorial service.

Help and encourage survivors to obtain professional grief counseling as soon as possible: Include all members of the immediate family, especially children.

Encourage counseling with someone who is sensitive to their faith and not familiar with the family. It allows more freedom to express thoughts and feelings without fear of being judged.

Gently caution the survivor against making any major decisions without seeking counsel first.

Provide continual reassurance that you will be there for them and they will make it through.

When Helping Suicide Survivors:

Have a balanced perspective on God's forgiveness, grace, and mercy. Survivors may be thinking about suicide, heaven and hell. Never tell or indicate to them that their loved one has gone to hell.

Initially survivors will have difficulty reaching out for themselves; you must reach out to them. Don't tell them to call you if they need anything; you call them.

Be prepared to give support and encouragement for one to two years, often longer. The more intense support will be within the first year.

Provide continual reassurance that God is still with them. Suicide survivors may feel that God has abandoned them as well.

Allow suicide survivors to express their anger at God, as well as their loved one.

Don't be shocked or offended by the survivors' emotional state and outpouring of anger, frustration, and tears. Be accepting.

Just your listening without saying anything in return is often what survivors needs the most. Someone's presence in silence is often enough.

Survivors may want to share their story repeatedly. Don't change the subject when they talk about their loved one, because it brings healing.

Be prepared for many questions you will not be able to answer. "Pray and comfort them with words of scripture without preaching or using religious cliches as a means of stifling the expression of grief."[1]

Don't criticize survivors for not going to church; however, encourage them to participate in worship services. It is often difficult to go to church when there is such a large void.

Don't let survivors sit alone when they do come to church. Show your love and support by your presence.

It is okay to speak of the lost loved one. It is often therapeutic and healing for survivors to share their memories, both good and bad.

When the survivor is ready, he/she may need help reintegrating into daily life activities. Confidence and self-esteem is a major part of the restoring and healing process.

Encourage survivors to become involved in activities again when you see them beginning to move on with their lives.

Don't discourage grieving rituals. Participation in religious rituals can help bring closure after a loved one's suicide.

Organizations for Referral and Resource Information

American Association of Suicidology
http://www.suicidology.org/
4201 Connecticut Ave., N.W. Ste. 408
Washington, DC 20008
(202) 237-2280

Friends for Survival Inc.
http://www.friendsforsurvival.org/
P.O. Box 214463
Sacramento, CA 95821
(916) 392-0664 — office number

American Foundation for Suicide Prevention
http://www.afsp.org
120 Wall St. 22nd Floor
New York, NY 10005
(212) 363-3500
Toll-Free: 1-888-333-AFSP

SA/VE (Suicide Awareness/Voices of Education)
http://www.save.org
7317 Cahill Road, Suite 207
Minneapolis, MN 55439-2080
(952) 946-7998

SPAN*USA* (Suicide Prevention Action Network USA, Inc)
http://www.spanusa.org
P.O. Box 73368
Washington, DC
20056-3368

SIEC (Suicide Information & Education Collection)
http://www.suicideinfo.ca/
Suite 320, 1202 Centre Street S.E.
Calgary, AB T2G 5A5
Phone: 403-245-3900
Fax: 403-245-0299

National Organization for People of Color Against
Suicide - NOPCAS:
1-866-899-5317
http://nopcas.com/

Yellow Ribbon Suicide Prevention Program
http://www.yellowribbon.org/

National Suicide Crisis Hotline Numbers
http://suicidehotlines.com/

––––––––––––––––––––

Letters to the author can be sent c/o:
The Father's House International
2165 Lucretia Avenue
San Jose, CA 95122
E-mail: newdaydawning@sbcglobal.net

References

Collins, G. R. (1988). *Christian counseling.*
Dallas: Word Publishing.

Fine, C. (1997). *No time to say goodbye; Surviving the suicide of a loved one.* New York: Doubleday.

Grollman, E. (1995). *Living when a loved one has died.*
Boston: Beacon Press.

Lawrenz, M., & Green, D. (1995). *Life after grief.*
Grand Rapids: Baker Books.